Sports Car
and
Competition Driving

Other books by the same author:

On the Starting Grid
Starting Grid to Chequered Flag
The Racing Porsches: A Technical Triumph
Porsche Racing Cars of the 70s
Porsche 911 Story

Patrick Stephens Limited, a member of the Haynes Publishing Group, has published authoritative, quality books for enthusiasts for a quarter of a century. During that time the company has established a reputation as one of the world's leading publishers of books on aviation, maritime, military, model-making, motor cycling, motoring, motor racing, railway and railway modelling subjects. Readers or authors with suggestions for books they would like to see published are invited to write to: The Editorial Director, Patrick Stephens Limited, Sparkford, Nr Yeovil, Somerset, BA22 7JJ.

Sports Car
and
Competition Driving

By Paul Frère

Foreword by Phil Hill

Patrick Stephens Limited

ISBN 1 85260 438 7

First published 1963

This second edition published 1993

© 1993 Paul Frère, Robert Bentley Inc.,

This edition published by: Patrick Stephens Limited,
part of the Haynes Publishing Group P.L.C., Sparkford, Nr. Yeovil, Somerset, BA 22 7JJ

Original edition published in the USA in 1992 by
Robert Bentley, Publishers
1000 Massachusetts Avenue
Cambridge, Massachusetts, 02138, U.S.A.

Printed in the United States of America

A catalogue record for this book is available from the British Library

Table of Contents

Foreword 6

Preface 9

CHAPTERS

CHAPTER 1   Basics 11

CHAPTER 2   Racing On Road and Track 30

CHAPTER 3   Cornering .35

CHAPTER 4   From Slipping To Sliding 51

CHAPTER 5   From Theory To Practice 73

CHAPTER 6   Practicing, Qualifying, Racing 82

CHAPTER 7   The Race 103

CHAPTER 8   Speed and Safety 111

CHAPTER 9   How To Become A Racing Driver 125

CHAPTER 10   Dos and Don'ts 130

APPENDICES

APPENDIX I   The Effect of Banking Angle and Tire Load on
               Maximum Cornering Speed 135

APPENDIX II   The Effect of Down Force on Maximum
               Cornering Speed 139

APPENDIX III   The Effect of All-wheel Drive on Handling 143

               Index 149

               Photo Credits 154

               About the Author 155

Foreword

Even though we did something as gregarious as driving race cars, I think there was a certain shyness on both our parts. We came from such different backgrounds: Paul the Belgian with the classical education, I the American who hadn't quite finished college. I don't think we quite knew what to make of each other when we first met in the early 1950s. It was at Le Mans, where we would eventually both meet with success. Paul wore those funny shorts. American men didn't wear shorts back then; it was a cultural thing.

These days, I look forward to every opportunity I have to see Paul Frère. Even now, 40 years later, the venue might well be a race track, or one of the *Road&Track* test sessions in Europe where we still get a chance to exercise our competitiveness—though in a very friendly, complementary manner. Every time I meet Paul Frère again, I am struck by what an international treasure he is.

Is that an odd way to describe a man? Think about this: can there be anyone else who has Paul's depth of knowledge and understanding of automobiles? I am fortunate to work in a business where I still drive cars—generally vintage machines—for a living, but I don't hold a candle to Paul's experience. His amazing memory bank contains personal driving data on such diverse machines as a 1953 Oldsmobile, a Lancia D50 Grand Prix car, DKW, a Porsche Indy 500 machine, a Ferrari F40—how long must that list be? But it isn't just quantity of knowledge, but also quality. Paul's analytical mind seems to filter out the trivia and retain only the important information.

I suspect that Paul has this all so well stored because although he was a top-notch racing driver—world class—he was never going to be a Grand Prix champion. Mixed in with all his talent, Paul had, for a young driver, an uncommon measure of rationality, common sense and maturity. Being a Grand Prix driver involves driving right there on the edge, with a willingness to occasionally step over that edge—a step that often proves fatal. I know how reluctant I was to be drawn over that line, and I've always suspected

Paul's nature made it even more difficult for him. Thank goodness. This re-
serve may have allowed Paul to live through what was probably the most
deadly period in auto racing history so that he could bring his experience to
his writing today.

Please don't take what I've just said as anything other than highly com-
plimentary. Paul may not have had the official title of World Driving Champion, but who would deny him the unoffical crown as champion driver of
the world? For Paul is respected not just by the racing community for his
years on the track, but he's even more highly regarded by chief engineers
from automobile companies worldwide. These executives may employ drivers and engineers in their thirties and forties to design and test their new
cars, but many of them still love to hear this septuagenarian's opinion. It's
like a final stamp of approval. I know that when he and I compare notes on
the cars we drive for *Road&Track*—some at over 200 mph (how many men
in their mid-70s do that on a regular basis!)—I'm always happy to find we
agree on many of the same attributes or deficiencies of the cars.

It is the analytical ability of Paul the engineer matched to the percep-
tion of Paul the race driver that make *Sports Car and Competition Driving*
such a valuable book. I agree completely with Paul's comment in his preface
that the very top drivers are naturals who were born with the ability to be
champions. But even for the talented driver there is so much to learn and
practice, and the book can be read on different levels by different drivers.

For the enthusiast drivers, who want to improve their abilities and get
the most from their automobile, Paul provides the basics for understanding
the fundamentals of performance driving and how it relates to safety on the
open road. Of particular help, considering the newest generation of 4-wheel
drive cars like the Porsche Carrera 4 and Dodge Stealth, is Paul's discussion
of the dynamic differences of chassis with drive to all wheels.

For the sporting drivers, who might try an occasional event, Paul takes
them a few steps further, dealing with everything from seating position to
the physics of cornering and handling. This can be of particular help to the
ever-growing ranks of drivers who have taken up vintage car racing and
might only compete in a race or two each year. A reading of *Sports Car and
Competition Driving* would be an excellent warm-up for each new season.

Serious young race drivers will approach Paul's book differently, I suspect. They might naturally be doing much of what is instructed in this vol-
ume, but it's where Paul the engineer takes over that he can help them relate
what they feel and sense as they drive to the actual physics and dynamics of
their race car. Considerable amounts of time can be gained on track by a
driver utilizing the countless lessons in this "textbook"—for example his

advice on the best shift points, based on a careful analysis of an engine's torque and horsepower. The appendices, on such diverse subjects as banking angle, tire load, and the principles of wind-induced downforce, illuminate physical laws that are not a part of raw natural talent but must be learned.

Many drivers may be too proud to read this book. They will assume they already know all there is to know about driving an automobile quickly. Big mistake. Driving any automobile, be it family sedan, turbo Porsche or Indy car, involves both knowledge and responsibility, and by reading *Sports Car and Competition Driving*, you can take a big step towards acquiring each.

Phil Hill
World Driving Champion, 1961

Preface

In the preface of the original edition of this work, written as far back as 1963, just after I had retired from racing, I wrote: "I do not believe that any book, or any amount of training of the kind given in competition driving courses will make a good driver out of anyone who does not possess a fundamental, inborn aptitude. Above a certain level, driving becomes a sport, demanding of its addicts instant and accurate reflexes combined with perfect judgement. In this sphere, only those who enjoy an outstanding natural gift and who take a profound interest in the subject will ever reach the top."

I have not changed my mind about this and I still don't believe that anyone as gifted as Juan-Manuel Fangio, Stirling Moss, Jim Clark, Niki Lauda,

The author (center) and Olivier Gendebien (right) being congratulated on the podium by the Mayoress of Le Mans after winning the 24 Hours Race in 1960.

Alain Prost or Ayrton Senna, to name but a few of the "greats" of the last 35 years, ever needed the help of books or race driving schools to rapidly emerge from the masses. Neither will established professional drivers learn anything from this book which they have long outgrown. Those I am addressing are the non-professionals who, as a rule, cannot devote much time to their motoring activities and who will surely benefit from all the experience that can be passed on to them, thereby reducing the time necessary for satisfying results to be obtained, in whatever type of competition they intend to enter. And as most of the principles applying to driving in competitions are dictated by physical laws, most of them also apply to driving on public roads, as long as they don't clash with the highway code. This is why, occasionally, some hints which have little to do with driving in races or rallies, but are useful for improving one's competence on public roads are given, while those with a more analytical mind will find a more detailed analysis of the basic physics governing the behavior of their car, of which a better understanding could contribute to making them better drivers.

The greater part of this book deals with racing, rather than rallying, simply because my own experience has been mainly acquired in circuit racing. But as the results of today's international and world championship rallies depend essentially on the performance achieved on a series of timed sections, to be covered in the shortest possible time, rallies have become, in fact, a series of sprint races. The difference to circuit racing is that they often take place on dirt roads or snow and ice which all afford much less grip than asphalt and consequently require a different driving technique, even though the physics involved remain basically the same.

The better understanding of these basic physics and of their influence on car behavior under the extreme conditions of racing should be of benefit to any driver seeking to improve his or her ability, even if he/she has no intention of taking part in competitions, and thereby contribute to greater safety on the road.

Chapter I

Basics

L earn to be a good driver first!
   Who is a good driver and who is not is a matter for discussion. Obviously, your family would not like you to drive them to the holiday resort of their choice in the same way you would drive in a big rally or in a race. One day, while I was away racing somewhere in Europe, my family was driven home from friends living out in the province by a quiet gentleman using

Fig. 1. The author driving a D-type Jaguar at Le Mans in 1957 when he finished fourth overall.

a big American car. Arriving home, the children said to their mother, "How nice it is to be driven in such a leisurely and quiet way; what a pity father doesn't drive as well as this gentleman!" But even if the sort of driving that is best suited to a Sunday outing is not exactly what is required of a racing driver, there are general rules that must be applied by both types—the observance of which distinguish the better from the not-so-good driver.

Driving Position

One of the basic requirements of good driving is a comfortable and purposeful driving position. Not many drivers are fully aware of its extreme importance, for it not only makes long journeys more comfortable but also improves the precision and the rapidity of their car control.

The body must be well supported, yet at the same time the position must afford complete freedom to perform those movements which are normally required in driving. The driver must be able to push all the pedals down firmly, without moving the body, and his right foot must be able to move quickly from the accelerator pedal to the brake pedal without the steering wheel fouling the knees. Ideally it should be possible for this movement to be carried out without moving the leg at all. The arms must be perfectly free to allow for movements of large amplitude.

In my opinion, the most important point about the driving position is that the distance between the driver and the steering wheel should be adequate. Most drivers sit too near the wheel because, when they were novices, they thought that by sitting near to the windscreen they could better judge the width of their car and see the road better, and they have never thought of changing this position since. In actual fact, it does not matter a bit if you can see the road a few inches nearer the car or not, and very soon a driver learns to know where the nearside of his car is without actually seeing it. The latter point, moreover, does not apply to most modern cars where the nearside is plainly visible however far back the driver sits.

If you make a driver sit farther back, he will most probably protest that he does not feel as safe as he did before. But that feeling will soon disappear and he will quickly become a better driver just because he is sitting in a better position. One of the reasons for this is that by sitting farther back he will not be able to brace himself on the steering wheel on corners. This will improve the precision of his control and will give him a finer feel of the road.

However, the main reason why a driver should sit well away from the wheel is that this position gives him a much better freedom of movement. From the normal position where his hands are poised at about "a quarter to three" on the steering wheel, he can turn it for roughly half a turn either way

Fig. 2. A correct driving position. The seat is adjusted to the driver to easily fully depress the pedals, while the seat-to-steering wheel reach is adjusted so that the elbows form an angle of approximately 120 degrees. The hands are in a position just over "quarter to three," allowing ample and equal movements in either direction without having to move the hands on the rim.

without the lower hand or arm fouling either the back of the seat or his body, and still keep complete control over the steering. For better sensitivity and precision, the hands should be lightly poised on the wheel, perhaps with one thumb holding a spoke for a safer grip, but never should the wheel be gripped tightly.

There is a strong tendency among drivers to use the steering wheel as a brace against the centrifugal force on bends and corners—a habit which prohibits any sensitivity for the steering. Instead, the driver should sit well back, and if necessary actually dig himself into the seat-back by pushing his body into it with his left foot, so as to get firm lateral support without the aid of the wheel.

In a racing car, the driver always gets much better lateral support than in a normal touring car, because racing cars always have properly designed bucket seats which are unsuitable for normal touring cars as they would make getting in and out too difficult. In addition, for safety reasons as much as for a better location of the driver in his seat, racing cars of all groups and classes are now fitted with a complete safety harness, firmly holding the

14

Driving Position

Fig. 3. *The distance to the wheel is crucial and should be such that when the wheel is turned by any amount, the driver remains in full contact with the contoured seat to oppose centrifugal force.*

Fig. 4. *Here, the driver is too far away from the wheel and his shoulders are not braced laterally.*

Fig. 5. If the driver sits too near the steering wheel, and this is turned over an angle of 90° or more, his lower hand is in an awkward position and the seat interferes with the movement.

Fig. 6. This shows the correct position.

Fig. 7. *The steering wheel should be held delicately, with the hands poised on the rim to provide a good feel. The thumb rests on the horizontal spoke and holds the hand in position without effort.*

Fig. 8. *A driver grasping the wheel vigorously, as shown here, is sure not to be an expert.*

driver in his seat. Such harness is required by international safety regulations to prevent injuries to the driver (and co-driver if there is one) in the cockpit designed as a survival cell.

Sitting back from the wheel can also be overdone. Never should the seat be moved so far back that the driver must actually lean forward in order to reach the top of the wheel, as this would reduce the lateral grip provided by the seat back. The position I personally prefer is the one in which, without leaning forward at all, I can just reach the top of the steering wheel with my arms almost fully extended. The driving position should never be dictated by the distance away from the pedals. With the seat properly adjusted in relation to the steering wheel, there is very little chance that they will be too close. If they are too far away, they can be adjusted in some cars. If not, it is usually very easy to modify them, if only by screwing blocks of wood on to the pedal pads.

Some road cars have an adjustable steering column which is a great help in obtaining the correct position and the correct distance to the steering wheel can, in most cases, be achieved by adjusting the seat-back rake while maintaining the seat in the optimum position in relation to the pedals.

17

Driving Position

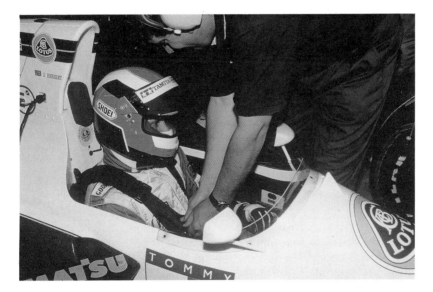

Fig. 9. If the car is fitted with a full racing safety harness, the driver is firmly held in his seat. If the steering wheel is too far away, its upper part is out of full reach.

Once the fore-and-aft position of the seat is properly adjusted, attention should be paid to its height. This should be chosen so as to give maximum visibility without raising the seat to such an extent that the steering wheel interferes with the movements of the legs, or the thighs with the movements of the hands. In some cars the seats can be adjusted for height, in others a properly designed cushion may solve the problem. If the seat is to be permanently raised, however, it is better to modify its mountings than to use a cushion which was not originally designed for the seat and which will probably make it less comfortable on long journeys.

Changing Gear

In the early years of automobiles, changing gear used to be the greatest headache of novice drivers. Modern synchromesh gearboxes, however, have simplified the driver's task to such an extent that anyone is now able to change gear, at least without making horrible noises. Nevertheless, the way in which a gear change is executed easily sorts out the good driver from the indifferent one. The difference lies much more in the way the clutch and accelerator pedals are used than in the way the gearbox itself is handled. It is well known that for a given road speed the engine runs at different speeds according to which gear is in use. Consequently, if a jerk is to be avoided when the driver lets the clutch in after he has selected a new gear, the engine speed must be adjusted accordingly, before the clutch is re-engaged. This is very easy when selecting a higher gear, for instance changing from third to fourth, as in this case the time necessary to move the lever from one position to the other usually just gives the engine a chance to slow down sufficiently for the drive to be taken up smoothly.

When a downward shift is to be made, however, the engine must be accelerated while the shift is being performed. Here, quite accurate judgement is necessary, as the engine must be accelerated by exactly the right amount if a jerk is to be avoided when the clutch is re-engaged. Moreover, if the down shift is being performed in order to increase acceleration or for climbing a hill, a smooth take-up can only be achieved if the engine is accelerated again while the drive is being taken up.

For this reason, in spite of modern synchronizing devices, many drivers continue to double de-clutch. This means that, when the gear lever has been moved into neutral, the clutch pedal is released for a brief moment while the engine is being accelerated before the clutch pedal is pushed in again and the next lower gear selected. This usually speeds up the engine by just the right amount for the drive to be taken up smoothly, besides nursing the synchromesh cones. In a racing car, double de-clutching is usually still a "must," as very few of them use a synchromesh gearbox. But with the close

Fig. 10. From theory to practice: the author, driving a Cooper Climax, sits well back with his left arm fully extended as he rounds a turn. (Brussels Grand Prix for Formula 2, 1960.)

ratios of non-synchromesh, dog clutch racing gearboxes and the low inertia multi-disc clutches used in most racing cars, the driver is usually content with simply easing the clutch while speeding up the engine and moving the shift lever, as is normal practice with motor cycles, which all use that same type of gearbox.

When to Change Gear

When to change gear depends very much on the objective. It may be maximum performance; it may be minimum consumption; it may also be minimum wear-and-tear on the car. These various aims call for differing techniques.

If minimum consumption is to be achieved you must remember that, in a gasoline engine, the specific consumption decreases as the load on the engine is increased. This means that under given conditions and for a given speed of the car, the engine uses less gasoline when it runs comparatively slowly—say in top gear—with a wide throttle opening than when it runs at a smaller throttle opening and at higher revolutions in a lower gear. It follows that to achieve the minimum fuel consumption, the engine must always be

20

Changing Gear

*Fig. 11. A perfect driving position illustrated by Olivier Gendebien on his way
to his first Le Mans victory, in a Ferrari, in 1958.*

kept at the lowest possible revolution rate without, however, letting it drop
into a range where efficiency is impaired. In this connection, it must be remembered that an engine's most efficient range of operation is the one over
which it produces its maximum torque. Below this range the efficiency falls
off and the specific consumption rises, because the valve timing is not
adapted to such low revolutions and losses occur due to scavenging of un-
burnt mixture and inadequate filling of the cylinders.

So, if maximum economy is the aim, gear changes must be performed
in such a way that the engine is kept working under a fairly high load in the
range where it produces its maximum torque, provided this does not result
in too high a maximum speed, when the increase in drag would offset the
engine's low specific consumption.

For minimum wear-and-tear the engine should also be kept in the mid-
dle revolution ranges, but not be given full throttle on a high gear unless it is
running at least at one-third of its maximum rotational speed, when the inertia forces partly offset the high gas pressure resulting from full-throttle op-

eration, transmitted to the bearings by the pistons and connecting rods. Very high rotational speeds, however, will result in very high inertia forces (which increase by the square of the rotational speed) with consequent high stresses on all moving parts. Slogging, or hard pulling, at low revolutions not only produces very high gas pressures but also may result in burnt valves while gas at high temperatures is laminated through them as they open and close comparatively slowly.

The main interest of the competition driver, however, lies in obtaining maximum performance. It is obvious that the higher the push the vehicle gets from its driving wheels, the faster will be its acceleration. The radius of the wheels being constant, the push will be proportional to the torque applied to the drive shafts. Neglecting the mechanical losses, this in turn will be equal to the torque produced by the engine multiplied by the gearbox ratio and multiplied again by the final drive ratio.

Thus, if the engine produces a torque of 100 lbs/ft which is put through a gearbox with a top gear ratio of 1:1 and through a final drive with a ratio of 4:1, the torque on the wheel drive shafts will be 400 lbs/ft, and if the wheels have a radius of 1 foot the resulting push will be of 400 lbs. In fact, due to mechanical losses, this will be about 10% lower, that is about 360 lbs. In the following discussions, however, for simplicity's sake, we will disregard the mechanical losses, which increase slightly with the increase of the transmission ratio.

It is often said and written that, when trying to obtain maximum acceleration, there is no point in pushing the engine above its maximum torque speed in the intermediate gears. This is entirely wrong, as is easy to demonstrate.

Let us take the example of a Porsche Carrera of which the engine produces a fairly constant torque between 4500 and 5800 rpm, with a maximum reading of 228 lb/ft at 4800 rpm. Fifth gear has a ratio of 0.868:1 and 4th gear a ratio of 1.086:1, while the final drive ratio is 3.44:1. Overall gearing is thus 3.74 in 4th and 2.91 in 5th, while the rolling radius of a rear wheel is 1.007 ft., which we shall simplify to 1 ft.

Disregarding the transmission losses (about 10%), the maximum driving force obtainable is

$$\frac{\text{Torque x overall gearing}}{\text{Radius of driving wheels}}$$

which, in 4th gear, is $\dfrac{228 \times 3.74}{1}$ = 853 lb., obtained at 4800 rpm.

If we change up into 5th gear at this stage, the engine revolutions will drop to $4800 \dfrac{2.99}{3.74} = 3837$ rpm, where the torque is 219 lb/ft. (see engine torque curve) and the driving force will drop to $\dfrac{219 \times 2.99}{1} = 658$ lb. Acceleration will thus be considerably reduced.

It can be easily calculated that the best change-up speed is just above 6600 rpm where the torque developed by the engine is 196 lb/ft. resulting in a driving force of $\dfrac{196 \times 3.74}{1} = 732$ lb/ft. Shifting into 5th at that stage will drop the revolutions to 5276 rpm where the torque available is 240 lb/ft, resulting in a driving force of 718 lb. The ideal shift point would be around 6620 rpm, when the driving forces in 4th and 5th would be equal. This is only 80 rpm below the maximum permissible engine speed. As the lower gears are more widely spaced than 4th and 5th (which is the rule in all cars), all other upshifts should be performed at the permissible limit if the best performance is required.

With engines which produce their maximum torque at comparatively low revolutions, say one-third of their peak power revolutions or less, it is usually beneficial to change up comparatively early, but that is never the case with racing engines in which the peak torque and peak power revolutions are usually close together.

Automatic Transmissions

Someone once remarked that automatic gearboxes work extremely well on cars which do not need a gearbox anyway. Originally, there was certainly some truth in this; automatic gearboxes were usually satisfactory only on high-powered and mostly expensive cars. This is probably why, at least in Europe, so many people found so many good excuses for not buying them. The most common excuse, of course, is that they are much too good drivers to rely on an automatic device for gear changing and much prefer to perform this function themselves. In my experience, this is wrong in about 90% of the cases, where the timing of the gear changes is much better done by an automatic device that also performs the shifts more smoothly. Moreover, modern automatic transmissions have a very high efficiency so that they waste hardly any more power and fuel than manual gearboxes.

Up to recent times, the only real problem with automatic transmissions was that they could not think and consequently had no foresight. All of them were so designed that when a lower gear is in use and the driver releases the accelerator pedal, they immediately shift up into top gear. This also applies to infinitely variable devices. On winding roads and especially on mountain roads, where fast driving calls for bursts of acceleration followed by braking periods, this is most inconvenient, as every time the car comes up to a corner the transmission shifts itself automatically back into top gear. When the accelerator is depressed again, precious time is lost while the engine is being accelerated and the downshift is being executed, while precise control of the power applied to the driving wheels is lost, which can result in sudden, and sometimes dangerous, wheelspin. Thus, if the best results are to be obtained with an automatic transmission, its automaticity has to be judiciously controlled by the overriding device with which all the better transmissions are provided, in order to enable the driver to keep a lower gear engaged whenever necessary.

Quite recently, thanks to the progress of electronics, "thinking" automatic transmissions have been developed in which the shift program is influenced by the way the car is driven. Sensors register the accelerator movements, car speed and lateral acceleration when cornering in addition to the more conventional inputs, and the data are processed in a computer controlling the shift program. Rapid movements of the accelerator pedal and high centrifugal forces indicate that a car is driven aggressively, and the transmission is monitored not to shift up before the engine has reached the maximum allowed revolutions and not to shift up if the accelerator is released for a short period, allowing the driver to retain full control of the power transmitted. No time is lost in unnecessary up and down shifts.

As automatic cars have only two pedals, it seems rather illogical to me to use the right foot *only* to operate both these pedals while leaving the left foot idle. Tests which I have carried out show that merely moving the foot from one pedal to another costs about one-tenth of a second, which is added to the driver's reaction time. Braking with the left foot, once it has been mastered, thus increases the safety margin as well as making town driving less jerky by smoothing out the transition from accelerating to braking—of which driving in heavy traffic mainly consists.

Many drivers, of course, will find that their left foot has not been trained to the sensitive control that braking requires. This is merely a matter of habit, which can be readily acquired by practicing on a quiet road. The main difficulty seems to face the driver who uses two cars alternately—one with, and one without, a clutch pedal. I personally have never found this to be a great problem, particularly if the two cars are of widely different types. It may be different, however, when two otherwise identical cars are driven in quick succession.

23

Automatic
Transmissions

Braking

Nothing is destroyed in Nature. The calorific energy contained in the fuel burnt by the engine is transformed into kinetic energy. While the car progresses, this is transformed back into heat generated in the car's various bearings, in the tires, and by air drag. All this heat is eventually absorbed by the surrounding air. Braking merely accelerates this process by heating up the brake drums or discs quickly so as to absorb more kinetic energy in a shorter time.

The main problem with braking lies in the fact that the heat generated in the brakes cannot be dissipated into the surrounding air as rapidly as it is produced, so that the brakes quickly become very hot. This discrepancy between the rate of production and absorption of the heat by the surrounding air is increased as the weight of the car and its speed rise for a given disc size. As the size of the brakes cannot be increased in proportion to the weight and the speed of the vehicle, fast driving on winding roads or in heavy traffic, involving frequent use of the brakes from high speeds, can produce very high temperatures indeed in the brake discs and linings. Temperatures can reach an even higher level when the brakes are used almost continuously, as in the long mountain descent for instance.

These high temperatures can produce brake fade, which is caused by the decreased coefficient of friction of the linings at very high temperatures. Racing linings are much less prone to fade—in fact usually have a low coefficient of friction when cold—but they usually require a higher pedal pressure and increase the rate of disc wear. Very high temperatures can also cause the brake fluid to boil with a resultant increase in pedal travel. This should be detected immediately by the driver, as a very small quantity of boiling fluid is enough for the pedal to go right to the floor without any effect; in contrast to the liquid brake fluid, the boiling part is compressible. It is particularly important that when the car has been stopped for a short time—up to 15 or 20 minutes after a drive in which the brakes have become very hot—the pedal is depressed for a check. When the car is at rest, brakes act as a heat sink from which heat spreads to the fluid contained in the calipers: brakes which were fully operative when the car was driven may have become totally inefficient after it has stood still for a while. It should also be remembered that brake fluid becomes aerated with time, which decreases its boiling temperature. It should consequently be changed periodically. Manufacturer's recommendation for road cars is usually once every year or two.

Of course, the brakes can be saved to quite an appreciable extent by using the engine as a brake, by changing down into a lower gear as soon as the car speed is reduced sufficiently to make this possible without over-revving the engine, and thus relieving them of some part of their work. This is a good safety precaution when driving down long mountain passes, but it increases wear-and-tear on the engine. So, unless there is a risk of fade, use the brakes rather than the engine for retardation. Brake pads are easier and cheaper to replace than engines!

It has been said more or less jokingly, that the less a racing driver uses his brakes, the faster he goes. This is of course true in so far as brakes never make a car go, and all unnecessary braking must obviously be avoided. But when a car must, of necessity, be slowed down, very heavy braking indeed is called for if the minimum of time is to be lost. Imagine a car running down a straight at 150 miles an hour towards a bend that can only be taken at 30. Obviously, it will reach the corner quicker if its speed of 150 mph is held until about 110 yards from the corner, when the driver will have to brake quite heavily in order to make the bend, than if the accelerator is lifted about 1,000 yards before the corner and the car is left to coast towards it relying mainly on the engine and the air drag for slowing down. In the first case, the speed of 150 mph is held up to the braking point only 110 yards from the corner, whereas in the second case the last 890 yards before the braking point are covered at a steadily decreasing speed. Nevertheless, of two drivers who can go equally fast, the one who uses his brakes less is the better one, and if it comes to an emergency he will be able to go faster than the other by using his brakes harder.

On ordinary roads especially, there is a lot of unnecessary braking that can often be avoided by some foresight, with a consequent saving not only of time but also of fuel, brake linings and tires. We will go further into this later.

One of the most difficult tasks with which a driver is faced is the judgement of the braking force that should be applied for prevailing road conditions, particularly on slippery surfaces. Except at comparatively slow speeds, the braking distance is increased when a wheel is locked. This means that to achieve the minimum braking distance from high speed, the brakes must be applied hard enough for the wheels to be just on the point of locking without actually doing so. If a wheel does lock, not only is the braking distance increased, but it also loses its ability to guide the vehicle, so that a skid can be induced. Locked front wheels make it impossible for the driver to steer the car, which is a frequent cause of accidents which could have been avoided by more delicate use of the brakes. The usual panic reaction of the average driver to such a situation is to apply the brakes even harder, which of course is anything but helpful. The correct reaction should be to release the pressure on the pedal slightly to give the tires a chance to re-establish their grip on the road. Admittedly such a reaction calls for quite a lot of practice, and it is not always easy to detect the exact moment when the wheels start turning again. If locking the wheels could not be avoided, then at least an attempt should be made to avoid the imminent accident, and the pressure on the pedal should be released at the last moment to unlock the wheels and attempt to steer clear of the obstacle.

Drivers who do not think they have the necessary sensitivity can use a slightly less efficient alternative method which leaves a larger margin for error. This consists of applying the brakes quite hard, then releasing the pedal slightly and then again depressing it harder and yet again reducing the pressure on the pedal. This gives the wheels a chance to unlock if the harder application of the brakes has locked them. This is exactly what anti-lock brake systems do. Only, electronics are much better than the best of human drivers. Not only do they apply and release the brakes in a much quicker succession, but they anticipate: they reduce the braking force before the wheel has actually locked and increase it again before it has actually resumed normal rolling, so that the wheel is kept rolling, but on the verge of locking, at a speed slightly slower than if it rolled freely. But it must be remembered that on rough roads, anti-lock brakes can seriously increase stopping distances.

Heel-and-Toeing

In order to save as much time as possible it is desirable that, after the car has been slowed down for some reason, maximum acceleration should be available as soon as it is required. This means that the proper gear should have been selected beforehand, so that the driver can call upon the highest available torque at the first touch of the accelerator. This also makes for safer driving as, especially in traffic, a burst of acceleration will save the situation as often as a hard application of the brakes.

When it is important to go fast, any major slowing down involves the use of the brakes. We have already seen that the later the braking point is left, the more time is saved. In many cases, when a car is driven in a spirited manner, a braking action requires a shift down into a lower gear, in view of the following acceleration. In order to make a correct down shift without causing a jerk and straining the transmission when the clutch is re-engaged, the engine must be speeded up during the process of the gear change. If the car is being braked at the limit and this precaution is not taken, not only will the transmission be strained, but also the driving wheels will tend to lock and may thus initiate a skid. With a non-synchromesh gearbox, the engine must be accelerated, and the double de-clutch technique must be used to avoid crashing the dog clutches. If, in order to achieve this, the accelerator

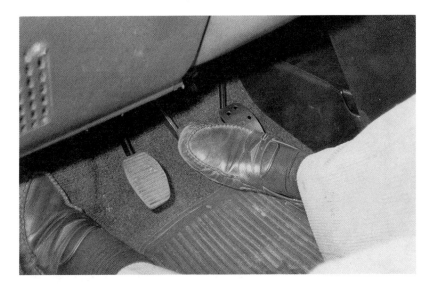

Fig. 12. "Heel-and-toeing" allows the driver to simultaneously brake and speed up the engine while making a down shift, with or without "double de-clutching," to adapt the engine speed to the lower gear and avoid a jerk when the clutch is reengaged. It avoids releasing the brakes to operate the accelerator and consequently reduces the braking distance, while complete control over the car is retained. Double de-clutching is essential with a non-synchromesh gearbox, as used in most racing cars, in an effort to reduce weight and because it allows quicker shifts.

pedal is to be depressed in the normal way, it means that the foot must momentarily release the brake pedal in order to actuate the accelerator. The car will thus be left to roll on, unchecked, in the braking area, all the time the brake pedal is left untouched. A jerky progress of the car will result, which may put it off balance, and the braking distance will inevitably be increased. On a fast approach to a slow corner, this increase may be quite significant.

Let us take the example of a fast sports car fitted with a five-speed gearbox, tearing down the straight of the Le Mans circuit at 220 mph towards Mulsanne Corner, which can be taken at only 40 mph and for which first gear must be used. If the driver wants to save his brakes to the utmost, he will successively change down into fourth, third, second, and first gear. Four changes—every one of which takes at least half a second—will thus have to be made while the car proceeds unchecked. The average speed of the car while it is being braked from 220 mph to 40 mph is 130 mph; at this speed,

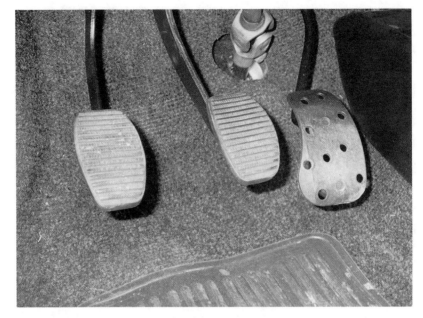

Fig. 13. In some sports cars, the accelerator pedal is specially shaped to facili-
tate heel-and-toeing, as in this Fiat Uno Turbo.

28

Heel-and-toeing

190 feet are covered in every second, so that during the two seconds the car
is left unchecked while the four downshifts are performed, it travels 380 feet
or just about 127 yards. This distance must, of course, be added to the actual braking distance, so that instead of leaving his braking point until, say, 200
yards before the corner, the driver will have to start braking at 327 yards, thus
forsaking nearly 130 yards of full throttle driving. This is why, with light cars
fitted with disc brakes and running in comparatively short races where brake
wear is not a problem any more, as is the case with the modern Grand Prix
cars, some drivers prefer not to go through all the gears on an approach to a
corner, but rather to nip from the gear they were in, directly into the gear required, without going through the intermediates. Even then, however, it is
advantageous to use the heel-and-toe method because it enables the driver
to depress the gas pedal, in order to double de-clutch, without releasing the
brakes.

This method consists of actuating the brake pedal with the ball of the
foot, which is left to exert its pressure on the pedal, while the heel depresses
the accelerator. Alternatively, and more normally, the brake can be pushed

down with the left half of the foot, which is tilted to depress the accelerator with its right half as required. The opposite procedure—actuating the brake with the heel and the accelerator with the ball of the foot—is to be avoided at all costs, as the heel is not sufficiently sensitive to provide the accuracy necessary for braking under difficult conditions. How far the accelerator is depressed on the other hand is not so important as, with the engine running idle, all that matters is how long the throttle is opened; how far it is opened makes very little difference.

Drivers who have practiced this so-called heal-and-toe method of gear changing will find that they can do it in most cars, and where it does not come easily the accelerator pedal can in many cases be bent to such an angle that the maneuver may be performed comfortably.

Not only does heel-and-toeing save time, it also gives such a sense of safety, due to the fact that the car is kept under the constant control of the driver, that even in ordinary traffic a driver accustomed to using this method finds himself very much at a loss in a car in which he cannot apply it. Passengers also appreciate the smooth progress that results from this drill. It makes starting on hills very much easier too, because the start can be performed without the use of the mostly inefficient and often inaccessible hand brake.

29

Heel-and-toeing

Chapter II

Racing on Road and Track

Apart from the ovals so popular in the United States, which are not what this book is about, racing circuits are designed to include bends of all kinds, as they are found on public roads. What I want to stress in this chapter is that there is a considerable difference between racing on a road that is not intimately known by the driver, and racing on a comparatively short circuit or track on which a certain number of practice laps enable the driver to learn well nigh every inch.

For maximum results, a circuit or a track leaves no room for improvisation. Pre-race practice has enabled the driver to get an almost photographic image of the circuit printed in his mind. He knows exactly what lies behind every blind corner; he knows exactly where to place his car on the road to get the best results; he has progressively found out how fast he can go through any corner and exactly where the limit lies; he has also found out precisely where to brake and where to change gear in order to round any corner or bend, or tackle any other hazard, at the speed practice has proved to be his, and his car's limits.

It follows that the essence of circuit or track racing is the ability of a driver to reach the absolute limits imposed by natural forces upon braking and cornering, to hold his car against these forces, and to repeat the performance lap after lap.

Racing on real public roads, as was best exemplified by the now defunct Mille Miglia, but which is still to be found in rallies in the form of timed special stages or in hill climbs, is a very different sort of racing that calls for a very different sort of ability. Here the driver has no chance to find out where the limit lies by proceeding gradually. Every corner, every bend, every hump-back creates a new situation which he must judge rapidly and accurately. This is the case even if—as is normally the case in international rallies—the location of the timed stages is clearly indicated in the regulations, making it possible for the crews to get some practice and to prepare the all-important road book. In the event itself, this is read by the co-driver, informing the

Fig. 14. Having prepared for the corner, Stirling Moss turns the wheel to full lock in a single smooth movement to take the station hairpin in the 1961 Monte Carlo Grand prix, which he won.

driver of every hazard coming up, telling him what sort of corner lies ahead and the approximate speed at which it can be taken. This notwithstanding, the need for improvisation remains high, since during the event the roads are closed to normal traffic, while practice obviously had to take place when the roads were open to the public—the driving method under each situation is different. Moreover conditions—if only the weather—may have changed drastically between practice, which usually takes place several days before the event, and the event itself. Consequently, not knowing the exact shape of the bend or corner lying before him, or the exact nature of the road surface or its profile, a driver who races on closed public roads must, of necessity, allow for any surprise and keep a small safety margin in hand. So, in contrast with the circuit or track driver, the rally or road driver's art is to judge as they arise a succession of new situations as accurately as possible, and consistently to reduce the vital safety margin to a minimum. His driving is thus more intuitive than scientific. He must also have a very highly developed sense of observation that will allow him to take advantage of anything that might help him to guess what lies ahead before he actually sees how the road is shaped. Anywhere the road disappears he will look for telegraph poles, trees, road signs, advertising posters, maybe the roof of another car or other things that might give him a clue to the shape of the road ahead. Always keeping in mind the necessity of observing a small safety margin, only occasionally and in an emergency will he reach the absolute limit of adhesion, as circuit drivers do on every corner and every time they brake on the approach to it.

While modern international rallies usually include timed sections on paved roads, some (as the Tour of Corsica) being run entirely on them, in many cases unpaved roads are predominant and these call for a very different technique which also applies to obtaining the best performance on snow and ice. In these cases, it is best to deliberately put the car in a four-

32

Racing on Road

Fig. 15. The author, driving a Ferrari in the 1955 Belgian Grand Prix, demonstrates how to cut a hairpin bend well beyond its apex, in order to straighten the line at the exit and accelerate the car quicker into the following straight.

wheel drift which is then mostly controlled by the accelerator. The theory of a four-wheel drift is explained in chapter 4, but an excellent description of a rally driver's art on loose ground is given by former world champion Walter Röhrl in the book *Quattro, der Sieg einer Idee* of which Herbert Volker and myself are co-authors:

> A rear-wheel driven car is steered with the accelerator. The steering wheel is used only to initiate the turn and to correct the line if the driver has been clumsy with the accelerator pedal. Accelerate hard and the rear wheels promptly start spinning, lose their cornering power and the car oversteers. Care should be taken to avoid too large drift angles, as forward motion is then excessively reduced. If you look spectacular, you are sure to be slow. The important thing is to strike the right compromise between wheelspin and lateral grip. The steering intervenes only to correct an excessive slide and prevent it from ending up in a spin.
>
> In a front-driven car, the front wheels which must drive the car as well as steer it, can easily be overstressed, resulting in understeer. To avoid this, the car must be balanced to make the rear end break away. This is done by going into the turn too fast and simultaneously releasing the accelerator and braking to transfer as much weight as possible away from the rear wheels. Operating the brakes with the left foot saves time and achieves the desired result in a hundredth of a second. Exiting the bend under power, the car inevitably understeers which makes front wheel driven cars unspectacular.
>
> A 4-wheel-drive car initiates a curve in a manner similar to a front drive model. It must consequently be turned into the bend in the same way by lifting off and braking—preferably with the left foot for immediate reaction—while balancing it into the turn. Exiting the bend, it also adopts an understeering attitude, but what happens in between is easier to handle. As soon as the rear breaks away, the drift is controlled by the accelerator, but less finesse is required than for a front or rear driven car, and it can be accelerated harder, as hard acceleration does not result in excessive oversteer as in rear driven cars, or understeer as with front wheel drive.

The question who is the greater, a great circuit driver or a great rally driver, could be debated for hours. Their specialties are so different that no fair comparison can be drawn between them. However, if I had to answer it, I would probably say that a great rally driver is the greater of the two, because his ability is exerted in a less artificial world than circuit or oval racing. His ability calls for constantly taking new decisions which must of necessity be

33

Rally Racing

right, otherwise he will lose time or go off the road, whereas pre-race practice enables the circuit or track driver to try for the limit progressively, as often as his likes, without taking great risks. On the other hand, circuit or track driving is a more scientific approach to driving than open road racing. Here the driver knows most of the factors of the problem to be solved, which is usually to take a bend or a succession of bends, including the braking area on the approach to them, as quickly as possible. If all the factors involved are known, it is even possible, with the help of computers, to calculate the fastest possible lap times on any circuit for any given car, or the possible time over any section. It has been done on many occasions and one wonders what is more admirable, the driver who manages to lap within less than a second of the computed possible lap time, or the accuracy of the computers capable of getting so close to the actual times obtained by top drivers.

34

Road vs. Track Drivers

Fig. 16. Richie Ginther (Ferrari), Graham Hill (B.R.M.) and Jim Clark (Lotus) take three different lines into a 180-degree bend. Ginther's is the "textbook line" while Clark adopts the "Moss Line," cutting in close right from the start of the corner. Ginther's line results in an increased radius in the second half of the bend and thus higher exit speed; Clark's line is shorter and permits later braking. In fact the various lines were probably chosen by the drivers in accordance with the handling characteristics of their cars: the strongly understeering front-engined Ferrari wants to be turned into the corner on the overrun and accelerated whilst its course is straightened, while the Lotus driver will manage to drive his car round the bend under power without excessive understeer. (Rheims, Muizon corner, 1960 French G.P.)

Chapter III

Cornering

I n this chapter we will try to lay down the main principles of cornering, based on the natural forces acting upon a car when the direction of its movement is changed. The ability of a car to be steered derives from the adhesion of its tires on the road. This adhesion is ruled by the coefficient of adhesion, which varies with the state and the nature of the road surface and is directly related to the weight of the car. This relationship is given by the formula:

$$A = W \times \mu$$

W being the car's weight and μ the coefficient of adhesion.

Under good conditions, μ for road tires on a grippy surface lies between 0.8 and 1.0 according to the main destination of the tire. In the case of racing tires, μ can be as high as 1.5, and even exceed it.

If, for example, $\mu = 0.8$, it will take a force of 1600 lb to make a 2000 lb car slide bodily sideways. If all wheels are locked, the same force will be required to move the car forward or in any other horizontal direction. As long as a car rolls forward in a straight line, its adhesion, which enables it to resist lateral forces, remains intact. As soon as it is being braked or driven, or as it changes direction, inertia forces are created which use up part of the available adhesion or "grip.".

Let us first take the case of a car that has already been driven from a straight line into a bend, and which now rounds it following a constant radius and at a constant speed. In this condition, the car is submitted to a centrifugal force:

$$F_c = \frac{m \times v^2}{r}$$

m being the mass of the car, v its velocity and r the radius of the curve.

This force is directed along the line going from the center of the curve to the center of gravity of the car. It can be broken down into two components, one acting rearward along the center line of the car, the other perpendicular to it and very nearly equal in force and direction to the centrifugal force itself as long as the curve is of comparatively large radius.

The centrifugal force being proportional to the mass of the car and thus to its weight (the mass being m = $\frac{\text{weight}}{\text{gravity}}$), it is also proportional to the vehicle's adhesion. Thus the lighter the car, the smaller the centrifugal force, which shows that the often-expressed opinion that light cars are more dangerous than heavy ones, because they are more prone to slide, is entirely false.

Of much greater interest are the two facts that the centrifugal force is 1) proportional to the square of the speed and 2) inversely proportional to the radius of the curve. The limit of adhesion at which the car will start to slide being reached when the main component of the centrifugal force (the one that acts at a right angle to the car's center line) becomes equal to the vehicle's adhesion, we find that by making the fullest use of the width of the road to increase the radius of the curve along which the vehicle travels, the centrifugal force will be reduced for a given speed of the car. A greater safety margin is thus provided, and the speed can be increased further before the limit is reached.

This is what is done in racing. The line of greatest radius that can be inscribed into a given curved section of road starts as close as possible to the verge of the road that lies on the outside of the corner, closes in towards the inside so as to put the car nearest the inside verge at the apex of the corner, then goes out again to the outside which is reached tangentially, when the car is straightened. In the case of a perfectly regular bend, the point where

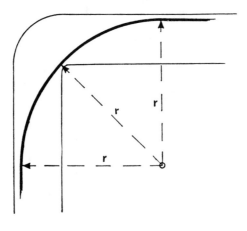

Fig. 17. Line of constant radius (r) inscribed into a right-angle corner.

the car comes closest to the inside verge lies exactly half-way through the corner. This, theoretically, is the fastest way through a corner, not taking into account the phases of entering the corner and leaving it which will be discussed later.

The aim of a racing driver, however, is not to drive as quickly as possible round any given corner or bend, but to lap a given circuit as fast as possible. Surprising as it may sound, this means that the bends and corners included in the circuit will have to be taken slightly slower than the absolute maximum they allow. This is because every bend and corner must be considered in conjunction with the straight, or straighter portion of the road, into which it leads. Every circuit is made up of bends, corners and faster stretches on which the car accelerates until it must be checked again for the next hazard. A straight is seldom long enough for the car to reach its absolute maximum speed; the progression of the racing car is thus mainly made up of bursts of acceleration followed by braking. If, to simplify the issue, we assume that the acceleration of a car along a straight is constant until the driver

Fig. 18. This Austin-Healey failed to cut the bend close enough and went spinning out of control when the driver tried to force it around along a too sharply curved line. (Production car race, Spa 1955.)

has to apply the brakes again, it is obvious that the faster the car comes into the straight, the faster will be its average speed along this straight up to the next braking point. For example, if one driver goes into the straight at 80 mph, and accelerates to 160 mph before he must brake again, a better driver who has gone into the straight at 85 mph, driving an identical car, will have reached 165 mph before he comes to the end of the straight. In the first instance, the average speed along the straight will have been 120 mph, in the second 125 mph. This is, in fact, not quite true in practice, as the rate of acceleration of a car decreases as its speed increases, but it shows that if the straight is long enough, the gain thus achieved may warrant a slightly slower average speed around the bend that precedes it, if this enables the driver to leave the bend at a higher speed and thus get a better run into the straight.

We have seen previously that the highest constant speed around a bend is reached by taking the line corresponding to the greatest radius that can be inscribed into the particular portion of road in question. For a given radius and coefficient of adhesion of the road, there is a corresponding speed that cannot be exceeded if the car is not to be pulled off the road by the centrifugal force. This in turn means that if the car is being driven round a corner at the maximum permissible speed, it cannot be accelerated until it has reached the end of the bend. In order to reach the straight at a speed higher than the maximum speed compatible with the corner, we must adopt a line that is different from the one resulting in the highest speed through the bend itself. This new line follows a curve of variable radius; at the beginning of the bend, the new line will be more sharply curved than the original line of constant radius that enables the curve itself to be taken at the highest possible speed; in the second part of the curve it will then progressively straighten up to a curve of longer radius than the original regular arc.

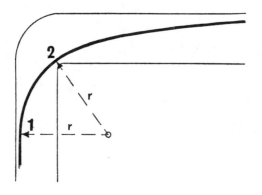

Fig. 19. Line of variable radius. The curvature remains approximately constant between 1 and 2, then flattens out.

38

The Line

Due to the sharper curve of the new line followed by the car in the first part of the bend, its speed will have to be reduced to a slightly lower figure than the one allowed by the original line of constant curvature. As soon, however, as it reaches the point where the curve starts to widen, the car can be accelerated as the progressive decrease of the curvature allows a progressive increase in its speed. The vehicle can thus be accelerated before it reaches the end of the curve, and the point before which it was not previously possible to accelerate along the line of constant curvature will be reached at a higher speed, thus giving a faster run into the following straight.

The advantage which results from using this method is quite easy to understand. Let us suppose that it takes the car about 2 seconds to round the bend and that it spends about 10 seconds on the straight before it must be slowed for the next bend: it thus spends five times as long on the straight as it does in the bend. If the line of variable radius taken through the bend costs 2 mph in average speed through the bend, but makes possible an increase of 2 mph in the average speed of the car along the straight, there will be a saving in time along the straight five times greater than what has been lost around the bend.

It will be seen that, instead of cutting the corner at its apex (that is, exactly half-way round the bend when this is of constant curvature), this new corrected line brings the car closest to the inside of the road at a slightly later moment. This closest point is moved along the corner towards its exit as the irregularity of the curvature of the line taken by the car is increased. Just how

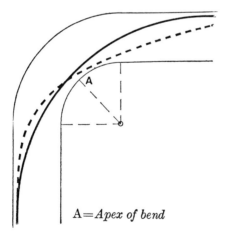

A=*Apex of bend*

Fig. 20. The solid line (constant radius) cuts the bend at its apex. The dotted line (variable radius) cuts the bend after its apex.

much the actual line to be taken should deviate from the ideal line of the greatest constant radius that can be inscribed into the particular portion of road under consideration, entirely depends on the performance of the car. If it has only just enough power to move it along the curve at the highest speed at which the bend can be taken, but cannot be accelerated any further, the ideal line of constant radius is the obvious choice. If, on the other hand, the car is capable of very high acceleration, it will be advantageous to increase the curvature of the line quite considerably upon entering the bend, in order to be able to straighten it in the second half of the curve so as to make full use of the car's acceleration. For a car with a performance between these

40

The Line

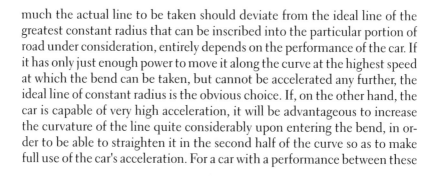

Fig. 21. If it enters the curve (at A) at the highest possible speed allowed by its adhesion, a car that follows the line of constant radius (solid line) cannot exceed this speed until the end of the curve is reached (at D). A car that follows the dotted line of variable radius must slow more to enter the corner, because its curvature is more accentuated. If the curve can be taken at 80 mph along the solid line, the speed of a car following the dotted line will be less at B (say 78 mph). But from C on, the car following this line can be accelerated. At D, its speed may already have reached 85 mph, when the car following the solid line is only just finishing its constant curve at 80 mph and can only now be accelerated. At E and F, and all along the following stretch, the car on the dotted line will be the faster.

two extremes, an intermediate line will give the best results. The benefit of taking a line of markedly variable curvature is particularly obvious on hairpin bends, which are taken by most fast cars in first gear, on which the acceleration is usually very quick.

This technique however can also be overdone, and in many driving courses too much emphasis is put upon the necessity of increasing the curvature of the line into a corner, the better to straighten it coming out of the corner, so that drivers end up turning into the bend too late, resulting in an initial curve that is much sharper than necessary, and then drive through the corner in a nearly straight line.

If a car is to round a corner as quickly as possible, it must, from the moment it is turned into the corner to the moment its course is straightened again, be kept at the limit of adhesion while using the entire width of the road. This means that the line it follows in the second part of the corner must only be opened up as much as the increasing speed of the car makes this necessary to keep it just below the limit of adhesion. If, in the second part of the corner, the course is straightened to the extent that full use is not made of the available adhesion, then time has been lost in entering the bend along a line of shorter radius than is necessary.

Driving Into and Out of a Corner

Up to now we have considered a car in the process of taking a curve of approximately constant radius and at approximately constant speed. We have neglected the inertia forces which take charge when the car is turned from a straight into a corner, or from a corner into a straight, and also every time the radius of the curve described by the car or the speed of the latter are varied. When a vehicle describes a curve, it not only rolls along a curved line, but also turns around its own vertical axis. A car running in a straight line has a rotational speed of zero around its vertical axis; when it rounds a turn of constant radius and at a constant speed, it has a uniform rotational speed and, but for frictional losses, would not need any outside force to maintain it. However, the car having a certain inertia around its own vertical axis, called polar inertia, a force is needed to produce the rotating movement when it is being driven from a straight into a curve. Conversely, a force of opposite direction will be needed to stop the rotating movement when the car comes out of the turn and into the straight again.

The best demonstration of the sort of forces involved can be made when a car is hoisted on a single-column lift in a service station. These lifts can turn round their own vertical axis which usually more or less coincides with the vertical axis going through the center of gravity of the car that is hoisted on them. If you try to turn the lift round you will find that quite a considerable force is needed to start it moving, but that once it turns, the force necessary to keep it on the move is quite small, as it is only necessary to compensate for the friction in the lifting mechanism. The greater force required to start the movement is needed to counteract the inertia of the car;

for a given leverage around the axis of the lift, the force it is necessary to apply is proportional to the rate at which the rotational speed of the vehicle is to be accelerated. Neglecting the friction in the mechanism, an equal force resulting in an equal torque around the lift's vertical axis (which we assume coincides with the vertical axis going through the center of gravity of the car) must be exerted in the opposite direction if the rotation is to be stopped at an equivalent rate of deceleration.

When a car is being driven from a straight line into a turn, a torque must be applied round the vertical axis going through its center of gravity in order to start it turning against its own inertia. This torque is created by forces acting through the contact points of the wheels with the road surface. Due to its inertia, the car reacts in the opposite direction so that at the start of a corner and as long as the radius of the curve into which the car is turned decreases, the reaction tends to pull the front wheels outwards and the rear wheels inwards. The reaction upon the front wheels being in approximately the same direction as the centrifugal force, if a car is turned too brutally into a corner this reaction, plus the component of the centrifugal force acting upon the front wheels, can add up to a total exceeding the adhesion of the front wheels, which may start a front-wheel slide. At the end of the bend, when the course of the car is being straightened up again, forces and reaction forces are reversed to stop the rotation of the car around its own vertical axis. The reaction upon the front wheels now tends to pull them inwards against the centrifugal force, whereas the reaction upon the rear wheels tends to pull them outwards and thus is added to the component of the centrifugal force acting upon the rear wheels. In theory, if the course if straightened up too sharply following a curve which has been taken near the limit of adhesion, a rear wheel slide could be induced.

The higher the polar inertia, the greater the forces required to make the car deviate from a steady course and vice-versa. Consequently, a car with a low polar inertia will be more affected by any disturbing force when driven in a straight line. It will be more "lively" than a car having a high polar inertia. It will also react quicker to any steering impulse, and racing cars are now all designed to have a low polar inertia, which is obtained by concentrating all heavy components (engine, gearbox, fuel tanks, driver) near the center of gravity. For road cars, such quick reactions are not always desirable, especially if they are aimed at the mass market and users who don't necessarily have the expertise required to deal with the reactions of a very lively car. It also makes a car more relaxing to drive on motorways, where straight line stability is a major requirement.

42

*Driving Into
and Out of a
Corner*

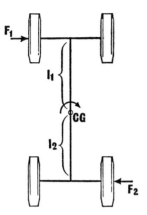

Fig. 22. To start a vehicle turning around its own vertical axis, a force must be exerted at the front and rear axles to create a torque $F_1l_1 + F_2l_2$. The wheels will react on the ground with equal forces but in opposite direction. These forces are proportional to the moment of inertia of the car around the vertical axis going through the center of gravity and they increase as the square of the acceleration of the rotational movement.

43

Driving Into and Out of a Corner

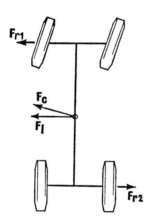

Fig. 23. When a car starts a turn, the lateral component F_l of the centrifugal force F_c acts in the same direction as the reaction force F_{r1} created by the car's moment of inertia at the front axle and in the opposite direction to the force F_{r2} created at the rear axle, thus tending to create a front-wheel slide.

But even a car having a low polar inertia cannot change direction instantly. It must of necessity be driven progressively into the curve and out of it, which in turn means that the line of the greatest radius that can be inscribed into the bend considered, cannot start and finish at the extreme outside verges of the road, as originally suggested. This also applies to the alternative modified line suggested, starting with a slightly sharper curve that is progressively straightened up in the second part of the bend. In both cases, the car must be steered progressively, but as quickly and precisely as possible into the curve which takes it off the extreme verge of the road until the line of proper curvature has been reached.

Transitory Turn

In fact there is a way of progressively driving the car into the turn, without leaving the extreme verge of the road before the car is following the line of proper curvature. Many drivers adopt it without actually realising it, simply because they do not like driving for any long distance only a few inches away from the verge of the road, until they get to a corner. As a result, on the approach to the corner they drive obliquely towards the outside verge, aiming their car at the point where it must be turned into the bend on to the line of proper curvature. In order to clear the verge towards which the car is driven, the turn must be started a little earlier than if the car were being driven parallel to the verge, thus making it possible for the driver to turn his car progressively on to the line of proper curvature, which is initiated at the exact point where the sweep comes nearest to the outside edge of the road - and thus without wasting any space.

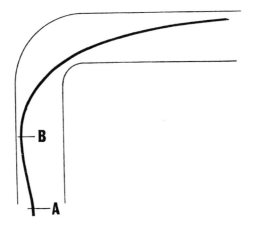

Fig. 24. The transitory turn (from A to B) leads the car progressively into the line of proper curvature, starting at B.

If he is determined to go really fast, an experienced driver approaching an unknown, fast corner which he cannot entirely overlook, will automatically find himself flicking the steering wheel to and fro in a quick succession of rather small movements. His aim— though, as they do it instinctively, very few drivers realise it—is to impart the car with an oscillating, snaking movement of small amplitude, but sufficient to start it turning to one side, then the other, so that it will turn more readily into the bend when the driver thinks fit to do so. In fact, the driver puts his car in a succession of small transitory curves, of which he picks the one that seems most suitable for turning the car into the bend to be negotiated.

Fig. 25. Illustrating the transitory line. Ayrton Senna's McLaren Honda has just initiated the right turn. The car in the background is on the line on which Senna approached the bend before closing up to the edge of the track at the turn-in point.

Succession of Bends

In accordance with the principle that it is more important for the car to leave a bend or a corner accelerating early and fast than to round it at the maximum speed, a succession of bends in opposite directions, following one another at too short intervals for the car to be placed correctly for each one to be taken individually, must be tackled in such a way that the car is correctly placed for the last bend to be taken at the highest possible speed. This will give the car the best run into the following straight. This means that the bend before the last must be taken in such a way that the car leaves it not on the outside but near the inside of the road so that it is placed correctly to take the last bend under the best possible conditions. The speed through the penultimate bend is thus sacrificed to the line through the last of the series. Through the previous bends, the line must, of course, be a compromise between making full use of the width of the road at the exit of one corner and placing the car correctly for the next one. The line to be followed depends solely upon the distance to the next bend in the opposite direction and the opportunity afforded to reposition the car correctly for it. A good driver always takes a perfectly smooth and flowing line along any piece of road—never an angular one.

Fig. 26. The correct line through an S-bend is illustrated by the two Williams-Renault of Riccardo Patrese and Thierry Boutsen. (Paul Ricard Circuit, French G.P., 1990.)

46

Road Camber

Taking Advantage of Road Camber (see also Appendix I)

Up to now, we have been assuming that the road was a perfectly flat and level surface. This is usually true only of aerodrome circuits. Ordinary roads are normally slightly domed, in order to allow water to drain away, so that the inside of bends is inclined inwards, forming a sort of banking, and on modern, properly engineered highways bends are banked on their entire width.

Such a banking allows a considerable increase of the car's speed through the bend, as figures 27 and 28 will show. In order to simplify matters, we will assume that the vehicle is driven on a road surface giving exceptional grip, equivalent to a coefficient of adhesion=1. This means that the adhesion of the car on a level road is equal to its weight W.

Let us first assume the car to be stopped on the banking, when the weight W can be broken up into a lateral force, parallel to the plane of the road, F_{lw}, and a force parallel to the vertical axis of the car (i.e. perpendicular to the road surface) F_{vw}. This force F_{vw} being less than W, it follows that the inclination of the road reduces the adhesion of the vehicle by the amounts $W - F_{vw}$. On the other hand, the lateral component tends to pull the car down the banking and will actually succeed in doing so if the angle of the banking reaches 45 degrees (or less if the coefficience of adhesion were less than 1, which it usually is).

If the car is now set moving round the bend, another set of forces will be created, originated by the centrifugal force F_c. This can again be broken up into a lateral force F_{lc}, acting parallel to the road surface, and a force parallel to the vertical axis of the car (i.e. perpendicular to the road surface) F_{vc}. The steeper the banking, the smaller the lateral force F_{lc} becomes for a given centrifugal force F_c, and the greater becomes the component F_{vc} which increases the adhesion of the car on the road

In competition driving, we are interested only in fast cornering giving rise to high centrifugal forces, in which case:

(a) F_{vc} is always greater than $W-F_{vw}$, which means that the adhesion of the car on the road is increased, enabling it to be cornered faster.

(b) F_{lc} is not only smaller than the centrifugal force F_c itself, but is counteracted by F_{lw}, so that the resultant force tending to pull the vehicle outward is considerably less than the centrifugal force which would act upon the car on an unbanked corner.

The overall result is that, on a banked corner, the increased adhesion and—for a given speed—reduced lateral force allow the car to be driven considerably faster round a bend of a given radius, even if the banking angle is only a few degrees. The driver must naturally try to take full advantage of this and eventually choose his line accordingly.

If, for instance, the road has a domed profile, resulting in all adverse camber on the outside of the bend, of which the adverse effect upon the adhesion of the vehicle is as marked as the correct camber is beneficial, the extreme outside of the bend must be avoided at all costs and the road must be treated as if it were narrower than it actually is. Moreover, the curve of the line taken through the bend must be adapted to the change of the banking angle, first being increased as the car gets nearer to the inner verge, then decreased as, beyond the apex of the bend, it is driven back towards the center of the road.

The profile of a correctly engineered bend, featuring a steeper but still comparatively small banking angle at the outside of the bend than on the inside calls for an entirely different technique. In this case, the sharpest turns are taken at the beginning and at the end of the bend, when the car is nearest the outside verge where the banking angle is steepest, while the curve is straightened when the car reaches the inside of the bend, where the road is flattest.

It is sometimes difficult for drivers without competition experience to appreciate how important it is to look out for any variation in the profile of the road and take advantage of it, but icy conditions vividly illustrate this, when, on a slightly domed road, the car can be taken round a curve, along

47

Road Camber

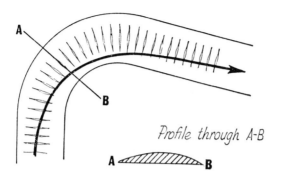

Fig. 27. Road with a domed profile.

Profile through A-B

48

Road Camber

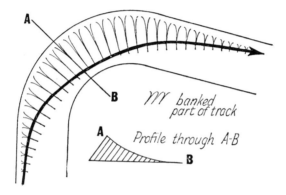

Fig. 28. Correctly engineered bend.

banked part of track

Profile through A-B

the inner verge, at a speed which would be quite impossible if it were driven on the crown of the road.

So far, we have dealt only with slightly banked curves, as are found on normal roads or road racing circuits. The long and steep banked curves, usually forming a complete semi-circle, used to connect the two straights of a racing or test track, such as those at Montlhéry and most proving ground speed tracks, call for an entirely different technique. On a track of this description, only a very slight increase of the radius of the curve described by the car can be gained by the usual cornering technique of entering the curve wide, cutting it at its apex and leaving it wide again, while cutting it at its apex implies that the car must be driven over an almost horizontal part of the track, instead of making use of the banking all the way round the curve.

On a properly designed steep banking, a car can be driven at very high speed without being subject to any lateral force tending to make it slide and deviate from its line. In order to achieve this, the driver must hold it on a

Fig. 29. The author instructing a Porsche driver in a competition driving course to cut into the gutter with the inside front wheel, in order to shorten the curve and to create a banking effect as the car leans into the lower level of the gutter.

Fig. 30. Olivier Gendebien's Ferrari on the banking at Montlhéry. Close observation of the picture will show that the suspension is about fully compressed by the centrifugal force pushing the car down on the track.

line where, at the particular speed adopted, the angle of the banking is such that the lateral components F_{lw} and F_{cw} created by the weight of the vehicle and by the centrifugal force respectively, cancel each other out (see Appendix I). This line is not only the safest, as it rules out any possibility of a slide, but is also the fastest, as it eliminates all power-absorbing side thrust on the tires, though with slow cars, which must be kept on a low line on the banking, the fastest line may sometimes lie somewhere between the no side-thrust line and the shortest round the curve, i.e. its extreme inside.

Owing to the fact that a car subjected to a sideways force tends to deviate in the direction of this force, it is very easy for the driver to find the line on the banking along which, at the speed reached by his car, all sideways forces cancel each other out. He must hold the steering wheel very lightly and let the car settle where it is pulled neither outwards by centrifugal action, nor inwards by gravity. In other words, the car must be left to find the correct line itself. All the driver has to do then is to drive it from the straight into the banked curve along a line corresponding the correct position of the car on the banking, so that it will not have to be driven up or pulled down, once it is in the curve.

As on a banked track the faster cars must be driven higher up the banking, slower cars must always be overtaken from above.

If, on a properly designed banked track, lateral forces tending to pull the car off its line can be entirely canceled out, another difficulty arises at high speed. This is due to the component of the centrifugal force F_{vc} acting perpendicularly to the track. It increases the force with which the vehicle bears upon the road, and is equivalent—as far as the strain put on the tires, the wheels, the suspension and the chassis frame is concerned—to an increase in the weight of the vehicle.

It can be calculated that, when the lateral forces cancel out on a curve with a banking of 45 degrees (i.e. when the centrifugal force is equal to the weight of the car), the total force with which the car bears upon the road is about 1.4 times its own weight. This condition is reached, for a curve of 250 metres (820 feet) radius, at a speed of 178 kph (111 mph). If, for the lateral forces to cancel out, the car must be driven higher up the banking, the force pushing it down on the road is notably increased. For a centrifugal force equal to twice the weight of the car, a banking angle of 64 degrees is required and the force with which the car bears upon the road is increased to as much as 2.25 times its own weight. For a curve of 250 metres (820 feet) radius, this condition is reached at a speed of 252 kph (157 mph), which can be dangerous if the suspension components and the tires are not suitably adapted.

Chapter IV

From Slipping to Sliding

S lipping
If a wheel and tire are allowed to roll without any lateral force acting upon them, they will roll in a straight line that lies in the plane of the wheel. Any force acting at a right angle to the plane of the rolling wheel will deflect it in the direction of the force applied. If this force is less than the adhesion of the wheel on the road, there will be no sliding of the tire on the road; the deviation will be due entirely to the deformation of the tire. This deviation, which, up to a certain point, is proportional to the sideways force acting upon the wheel and tire, is called the "slip"—as opposed to a "slide," which takes place when the limit of adhesion has been exceeded. The angle included between the plane of the wheel and the path it follows under the action of the sideways force acting upon it is called the slip angle. The deviation is caused by the lateral deflection of the tire under the force that pushes it sideways. Due to this deflection, the path of the tread of the rolling tire that is not in contact with the ground is not in line with the center of the contact surface; it is deviated some distance in the direction of the force acting upon the wheel. When some part of that free tread comes into contact

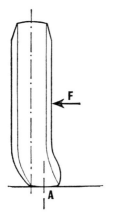

Fig. 31. When a force F is applied at a right angle to the plane of the wheel, the tire deflects and the center A of its contact surface with the road is not in line with the wheel's vertical plane of symmetry.

with the ground, the center of its contact surface will thus not be in the same alignment as the center of the contact surface previously considered. A good idea of what actually happens can be obtained by rolling a circular eraser, such as is used for typewriting, on a table and at the same time pushing it laterally while it is held down firmly enough on the table to prevent skidding.

Thus under the influence of a lateral force, such as is produced by the centrifugal force acting upon a car, a rolling wheel and tire will deviate from its plane without actually sliding. As a result, even without skidding and at comparatively low speed, a car rounding a corner will not follow the exact path indicated by the geometry of its wheels. The actual geometry of the turn will be given by the actual path followed by the wheels, taking into account their slip angle. Any increase or decrease of the slip angle will modify the path followed by the vehicle, having the same effect as a modification to the orientation of the wheels. This form of steering is of course done by the rear wheels as well as by the front wheels of the vehicle. For a given tire, the slip angle is mainly dependent upon four factors:

1) The sideways force acting upon the wheel. Any increase of this force will obviously increase the slip angle.

2) The tire pressure. Any increase of the pressure in the tire will decrease its lateral flexibility and thus reduce the slip angle; conversely, any decrease in the pressure will augment it.

3) The weight carried by the tire. For a given lateral force, the slip angle of a tire is at its minimum around the weight for which the tire has been designed. Increasing or decreasing the weight by any considerable amount will augment the slip angle. In the case of decreasing weight, this is partly due to increased scrub.

52

Slipping

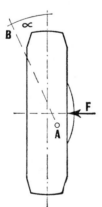

Fig. 32. Plan view of rolling wheel submitted to a force F applied at a right angle to its plane (lateral force). The center of the contact point of the tire with the road (A) is offset to the side and to the rear. The angle α is the slip angle. Instead of following the direction of its own plane, the wheel is deviated along the line AB.

4) The camber of the wheel. Positive wheel camber increases the slip angle under given conditions, whereas, up to a certain limit, negative camber reduces it.

Sliding

The slip angle reaches a maximum when the lateral force acting upon the wheel approaches the tire's grip on the ground. When the adhesion is exceeded, the slip is turned into a slide, when the tire actually scrubs over the road. Obviously the angle of slide is added to the angle of slip.

Whereas slipping can only be provoked by a force acting in a perpendicular direction to the plane of the wheel, sliding can also be induced by forces acting in the same plane as the wheel, that is, by braking or driving forces.

The adhesion of the tire on the road is the same in all directions. This means that if we want to pull a locked wheel in its own plane, we will have to exert the same force as is needed to move it sideways or in any other direction. Similarly, if torque is applied to the wheel, the driving force acting upon the ground cannot exceed the adhesion of the wheel.

The important fact in this connection is that any amount of grip used up by a driving or braking force reduces the resistance with which the wheel can oppose a force acting perpendicularly to its plane. The constancy of the adhesion in all directions can be represented diagrammatically by a circle which has its center at the contact point of the tire with the road. The radius of this circle gives the measure of the force of adhesion. If a force greater than the radius of the circle is applied in any direction at the contact point of the tire with the road, the tire will slide; if the force applied is less than the

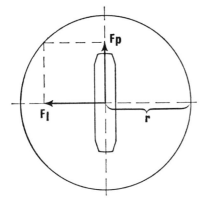

Fig. 33. r is the measure of the tire's adhesion on the road. If a force F_l acts laterally upon the wheel, F_p remains available to propel the vehicle or, conversely, for braking. If a driving or braking force F_p is applied, any lateral force greater than F_l will produce a slide. F_l is thus the maximum lateral adhesion available against sliding when a driving or braking force F_p is applied through the contact surface of the tire with the road. Total adhesion $= \sqrt{F_p{}^2 + F_l{}^2}$

radius of the circle, it will not move. All forces applied to the contact point (for the sake of simplicity we will consider that the contact patch between the tire and the road surface is a point) can be broken down into (1) a force acting perpendicularly to the plane of the wheel and (2) a force acting in the plane of the wheel. These two forces are interdependent; if a force less than the adhesion force is applied in the plane of the wheel (that is, a driving or a braking force) the resistance opposed by the tire to a force acting perpendicularly to the plane of the wheel (that is, to a force that tends to make it slide sideways) will be reduced. Conversely, any force acting at a right angle to the wheel plane (that is, a force that tends to make the car slide) will reduce its

54

Sliding

driving or braking power. These forces are related by the formula:

$$\text{Total Adhesion} = \sqrt{F_p^2 + F_l^2},$$

F_p being the force acting in the plane of the wheel and F_l the lateral force.

Thus, if a force F_p is put through the wheel to drive or brake the vehicle, a force F_l acting at right angles to the plane of the wheel

$$F_l = \sqrt{(\text{Total Adhesion})^2 - F_p^2}$$

will suffice to make the wheel slide. Consequently, if the wheel is submitted to a sideways force F_l, the maximum driving force it will be able to transmit without spinning will be

$$F_p = \sqrt{(\text{Total Adhesion})^2 - F_l^2}.$$

This formula shows not only that any force applied in one of the planes reduces the ability of the wheel to resist forces in the plane acting at right angles to the force applied, but also that if one of the forces is equal to the adhesion of the tire on the road, there will be no adhesion left to oppose any other force.

This means that if a wheel is spinning under an excessive driving torque or is locked in braking, it will not be able to resist skidding in any way; conversely, if the wheel is skidding, with no driving or braking force applied, it will not be able to transmit either of these if required. This explains why even an ordinary touring car that is being cornered steadily on a slippery road under a small throttle opening, will slide as soon as the throttle is opened wide enough in an intermediate gear to make the driving wheels spin. The power slide thus produced will stop only if the throttle is released enough to reduce the driving force to an amount compatible with the lateral force acting upon the wheel, or if the car is steered straight out of the corner so as to reduce the lateral force acting upon the wheel to a value compatible with the driving force applied. These are in fact the two means by which the driver can correct a skid. The exact point where, under the influence of an

Fig. 34. With cars running in close company, it is not always possible, or even desirable, to take the academic line through a bend. Here Willy Mairesse took what was probably the most desirable line into a 180-degree turn, but Luciano Bianchi has managed to nip into the inside and might just be able to force the leading car out of its line at the exit. Had Mairesse kept closer in he might have lost a few hundredths of a second, but he could not have been pushed off his line and would have been certain to stay in front. (Tour de France 1961, Brussels-Heysel Circuit.)

increasing lateral force acting upon a rolling wheel the slide takes over from the slip is very different to assess.

With narrow road tires, the transition is rather progressive and quickly increasing slip angles give the driver a fair warning that the limit is near and slide is going to take over from slip. The transition is much more abrupt with wide, high-performance tires, which tend to hang on, generating comparatively small slip angles until the limit is reached and slide takes over with little warning, calling for a quick reaction from the driver. Extreme conditions are reached in racing cars which, in addition to ultra-wide, high-grip tires, have a low polar moment of inertia.

Oversteer and Understeer

Whether a side force merely induces slip or causes the wheels to slide, the limit of adhesion having been exceeded, the practical effect is that the wheels roll at an angle to their own plane. Consequently slip and slide have a very similar bearing upon the car's attitude, changing the direction of travel independently of the driver's action on the steering.

While a car's behavior when the limit of adhesion has been exceeded on one or both sets of wheels is mainly dependent on the driver's action, the basic behavior is dictated by the slip angles generated by the front and rear tires when the car is submitted to a lateral force, be it centrifugal force when cornering, the force of a side wind or any other. When, under a certain lateral force, the slip angle of the front wheels is smaller than the slip angle of the rear wheels, the vehicle is said to oversteer because it actually makes a tighter turn that the one corresponding to the geometrical position of the wheels. If the slip angle of the front wheels is greater than that of the rear wheels, the car understeers; it takes a wider turn that the one corresponding

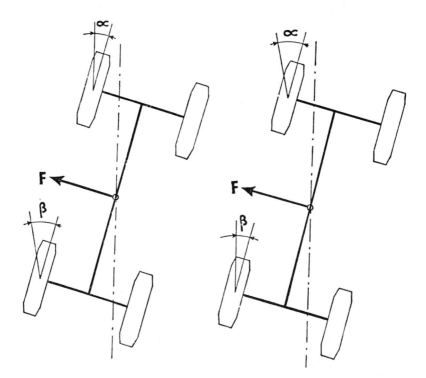

Fig. 35. *Oversteering car (left)* $\alpha < \beta$. *The front slip angle is narrower than the rear slip angle. The vehicle tends to deviate farther from its original line of progress. Understeering car (right)* $\alpha > \beta$. *The front slip angle is greater than the rear slip angle. The vehicle, deviated from its line, tends to turn back to its original direction of progress.*

to the geometrical position of the wheels. Equal slip angles front and rear will result in a so-called neutral-steer car. In practice, a neutral-steer car, that is, a car rounding a bend with equal slip angles front and rear, will not exactly follow the line dictated by the geometrical position of its wheels, but will describe a circle of larger radius. It would follow the geometrically defined circle only if the slip angles were nil, or if the car oversteered slightly.

The ratio of front to rear slip angle varies not only according to the car under consideration but even for one and the same car under differing conditions. Load for example will affect the handling characteristics. If a four-passenger car is fully laden, its center of gravity is moved rearward, so that the distribution of the components of the centrifugal force acting upon the front and rear axles is altered, a larger component acting upon the rear axle and a smaller upon the front axle. The rear slip angles will be increased and the front ones reduced, creating an oversteer tendency, further augmented by the increased load on the rear tires also inducing larger slip angles.

Knowing the factors influencing the behavior of tires when submitted to a lateral force, it is possible, up to a certain point, to influence a car's behavior by using front and rear suspensions of different geometries, appropriate roll stiffnesses and roll-steer characteristics, so that they will react differently when a lateral force acting upon the center of gravity induces roll. For example, up to a point excessive oversteer can be corrected by designing the rear suspension to produce some toe-in of the outside rear wheel when the car rolls, to compensate for the excessive slip angle. With a beam axle or with four-wheel steering, the rear axle can even be made to steer slightly to compensate for the rear slip angle.

But even if one wished to design a car possessing absolutely constant cornering characteristics, for example a car that would remain neutral whatever the lateral force acting upon it, it would be impossible to do so. The reason for this is that, under various circumstances, the forces acting at a right angle to the plane of the front and rear wheels respectively, do not always keep the same proportions. When it is being turned into a corner, a car will tend to understeer due to its own inertia; the quicker it is turned into it, the more will it do so.

For any given value of the centrifugal force, the component acting at a right angle to the rear wheels decreases more than the component acting upon the front wheels, as the radius of the corner decreases. Thus the sharper the corner, the less oversteer will be noticed and the more understeer will become apparent.

On a rear-wheel drive car, the driving force is always exerted by the rear axle along the longitudinal axis of the vehicle. As the front wheels are turned, the driving force creates a lateral component upon the front wheels

57

Oversteer and Understeer

Oversteer and
Understeer

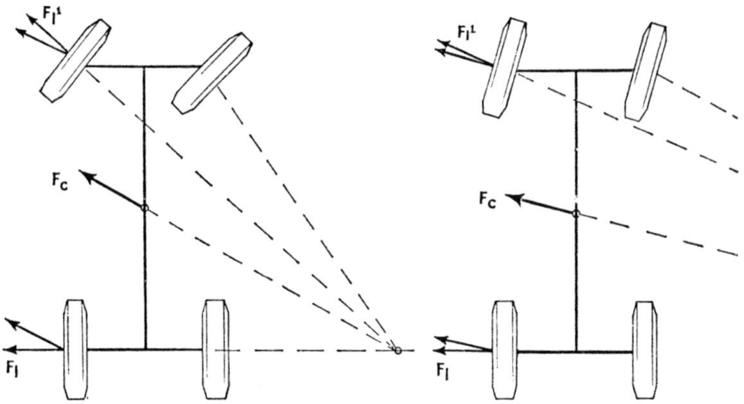

Fig. 36. As the radius of the turn decreases, the lateral component F_l of the centrifugal force F_c acting upon the rear wheels decreases more than the component F_l^1 acting upon the front wheels.

which becomes greater as the lock of the front wheels is increased (Fig. 36). This obviously creates an additional degree of understeer which is added to the normal tendency of an understeering car, or can even momentarily induce a basically oversteering car to understeer.

If, however, in a rear-wheel driven car, enough torque is put through the driving wheels to produce wheel spin while the car is cornering, the grip available to guide the wheels in a transverse direction is exhausted and the rear end breaks out, producing oversteer by "powersliding," whatever the car's basic characteristics. If it is not checked by lifting the accelerator and/ or unwinding the steering, the car will spin.

Front-wheel driven cars basically tend to understeer, if only because their center of gravity is nearer the front than the rear wheel axis, so that the larger component of the total side force affects the front wheels. If necessary, this can be corrected by appropriate suspension tuning, but the higher the driving torque transmitted through the front wheels, the less the grip available to resist lateral forces and the larger their slip angle. Whenever the front wheels actually drive the car (i.e. when the driver applies power), being at the same time submitted to a lateral force, they will reach their limit of adhesion (i.e. lose grip) before the rear wheels, and run wide. This is why, under power, all front-wheel driven cars are final understeerers.

Final understeer under power is also a characteristic of four-wheel driven cars, but in this case, a lot more power is required to break the grip, as the driving torque is spread over all four wheels. A more detailed study of the

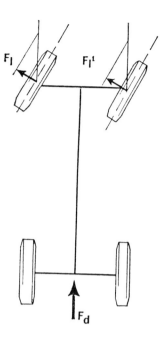

Fig. 37. In a rear-wheel drive car, the driving force F_d creates a lateral component force (F_l and F_l^l) acting upon the front wheels as these are turned into a curve.

59

*Turning
Understeer into
Oversteer*

behavior of 4-wheel drive cars compared to front- and rear-wheel driven models will be found in the Appendix section of this book.

Turning Understeer into Oversteer

An understeering car is a stable car whereas an oversteering car progresses in an unbalanced state. This is easy to understand: as soon as a car is deviated from its straight line of progress, a centrifugal force is created that acts upon the car and causes the tires to slip. The slip angle at the front wheels of an understeering car being greater than the slip angle at the rear wheels, the car will automatically tend to turn back to its original direction of progress. If, however, the car oversteers, due to the slip angle at the rear wheels being greater than the slip angle at the front wheels, the car will steer itself towards the direction into which it has been deviated, thus accentuating the deviation. This in turn will increase the centrifugal force acting upon it, the front and rear slip angle differential will be increased, and if the driver does not take immediate action, the car will turn into an increasingly sharper curve and eventually spin.

It is generally recognized that for the non-expert driver, it is best for a car to understeer consistently. He or she will never notice the understeer and simply adjust the lock to make the car go where he or she wants it to go. This is one reason why front-wheel driven cars are so popular: they make the driving unproblematic, as the driver hardly ever faces a situation where the steering must be unwinded to correct a rear end skid.

Opinions, however, differ on the behavior the car should have when, while cornering, the driver releases the accelerator pedal. Some manufacturers go to great lengths to tune the suspension to combat the natural tendency of the car to slightly turn into the bend, i.e. for the understeer to be reduced due to the weight transfer which unloads the rear wheels and loads the front, decreasing the front and increasing the rear slip angles. Others insist that the car should respond to lifting off by turning into the bend—but gently for the car to remain easily controllable. I am very much an addict of this latter school as, if the car turns into the bend, it helps the driver negotiate a bend he has approached too fast, while an expert driver will use this behavior to help the car quickly change direction, hence improving its agility on winding roads and in cases of emergency. I consider this behavior to be absolutely essential, especially for sporting front- and four-wheel drive cars for which final understeer under power is the rule.

While there is little to choose between a front- and a rear-wheel driven car when it comes to handling and the ultimate speed at which bends can be negociated, there is a limit to the driving force which can be transmitted through the front wheels. Front-wheel drive cars are reputed to have better traction than equivalent rear-wheel driven models. In the case of an unladen touring car, this is usually true, as in most front-wheel driven cars, more than 60% of the total weight is concentrated on the driving wheels. This is also true of rear or central engined cars with rear-wheel drive. But there is a rather low limit to the driving force which can be transmitted through the front wheels. This is because the faster the car accelerates, the more weight is transferred from the front to the rear axle. Consequently the more power is used to accelerate, the less the grip available at the driving wheels. This is why powerful racing cars are always driven by the rear wheels. In this case, the weight transfer which is proportional to the acceleration (and inversely proportional to the wheelbase and the height of the center of gravity) increases the grip available at the driving wheels as the torque increases.

For racing on hard surfaces, it is best for a car to slightly understeer, which is indispensable for stability on straights and, above all, in fast bends, but to respond by slightly oversteering or reducing the understeer whenever the driver releases the accelerator. This helps turn-in when negotiating a bend. It should also have enough power to break the grip of the driving wheels to produce controlled "power oversteer" at the exit of the bend. In this case the car can negotiate the bend in a four-wheel drift and be in line with the following straight—if any—even before the car has exited the bend. It can then be accelerated at full power benefiting from the full grip of the driving wheels, the side force having dropped to an insignificant level. To achieve this, it is essential to accurately control the amount of power oversteer produced, and in this connection the presence of a limited slip differential is essential. Otherwise, the inside driving wheel will spin, while the grip of the more laden outer wheel will not be broken and the rear end will not drift out of line when required.

Fig. 38. Driving a Porsche Turbo, the author demonstrates how a powerful rear-wheel driven car can be powered out of a bend to push the tail out and align the car for the exit of the turn before it has actually been reached. If the yaw angle is larger than this, time is lost.

The drift angles assumed by today's top racing cars are much smaller than those of racing cars of the 1960s, mainly because modern racing tires produce much smaller drift angles than those of yesterday (no more than 2 degrees) and because of the very high grip induced by the aerodynamic down force acting upon the car. But comparatively large drift angles can still be observed in touring car racing.

Fig. 39. This is about the largest drift angle modern single seaters will assume. (Alain Prost, Ferrari, 1990 in the French G.P., Paul Ricard Circuit.)

62

*Drifting a Car
Through a Bend*

Drifting a Car Through a Bend

While on loose and slippery ground, a front-wheel driven car can be drifted through a bend by using appropriate and sometimes freak driving methods on which we shall come back, the best configuration to achieve a proper and time-saving four-wheel drift is rear-wheel drive.

Drifting implies that, under the combined effects of the lateral component of the centrifugal force on the rear wheels and of the driving torque, the limit of adhesion is reached at the rear wheels before it is reached at the front wheels, which are subjected to the action of the lateral components of the driving and centrifugal forces only. In order to have the best control over the drift, it is necessary for the driver to have the greatest available torque that can be produced at the rear wheels immediately at his command. To achieve this he must select the proper gear before reaching the bend in which the car is to be drifted, so that the torque applied can be controlled precisely and immediately by the accelerator pedal. This is vitally important, as the drifting car is controlled as much by the driver's action upon the accelerator as by the steering wheel.

There is no clearly defined borderline between the so-called four-wheel drift and a proper slide or skid. In racing parlance, however, a car is usually said to be drifting when its front wheels are still more or less pointed in the direction of the bend to be taken, or, in marginal cases, are straight (Fig. 51); the slide proper starts when the driver has to correct the line of progress by turning the front wheels into the opposite direction to the curve to be taken. From this it follows that only an understeering car can be drifted, as in most other cases the rear slip and slide angles will add up to such a total compared with the front slip angle, that the front wheels will have to be turned out slightly to compensate for the difference. If they must be turned out so much that they point in the opposite direction to the bend to be taken, the drift is turned into a slide or a skid.

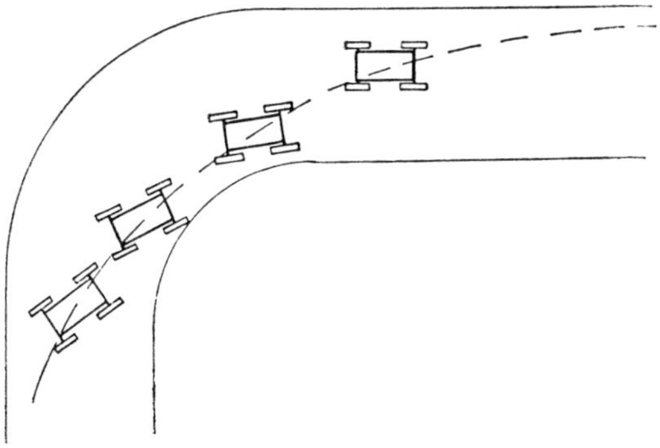

Fig. 40. The yaw angle formed by a car rounding a bend in a drift, brings the vehicle in line with the straight following the bend before it has actually completed the curve.

The drift is the position which a properly designed under-steering car assumes automatically when it is being cornered near the limit while sufficient torque is applied to the rear driving wheels—at least enough to keep up its speed. It is obviously dependent to a certain extent upon the ability and the judgement of the driver, but, within certain limits, it is a state of stable equilibrium. When a car rounds a curve at a speed low enough for the slip to be negligible, the center O of the curve it describes is in line with the rear wheel axis, where it is joined by the lines drawn at right angles to the plane of the front wheels. As soon as the rear wheel slip goes over into slide, this point does not correspond any more with the center of the actual curve taken by the vehicle. It moves to O_1 which lies ahead of the rear wheel axis. Figure 41 shows that if the car were moving around the center point O, that is without drifting or sliding, it would very soon hit the inside of the curve; in actual fact moves around O_1. This changes the direction of the centrifugal force from OG to O_1G, where it forms a much smaller angle in respect to the planes of the wheels. Assuming in both cases the value of the centrifugal force to be identical, the value of the component acting at a right angle to the wheel planes is reduced. It gives rise, however, to a comparatively important component acting in the plane of the wheels and opposing the rolling motion of the car, tending to slow it.

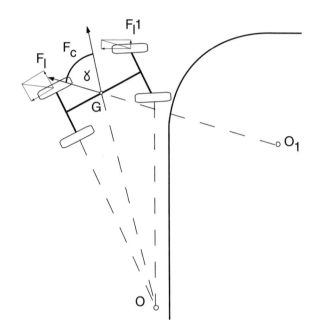

Fig. 41. Car in a four-wheel drift. The greater the yaw angle γ, the smaller become the lateral components F_l^1 and F_l of the centrifugal F_c acting upon the front and rear wheels, while the components acting backwards in the plane of the wheels are increased.

As long as the driver does not modify the steering lock or the torque applied to the driving wheels, the car remains in a state of balance created by the various forces acting upon it. If, for any reason, the rear wheels were to drift out more, which would happen for instance if the driving torque were increased, thus decreasing the resistance of the rear axle to lateral forces, the car would assume a greater yaw angle (γ), thereby automatically reducing the component of the centrifugal force acting at right angles to the plane of the wheels, increasing the component directed along their plane towards the rear and automatically slowing the vehicle. A new state of equilibrium is thus achieved, the greater torque applied matching the increased rolling resistance of the car, and the reduced lateral component of the centrifugal force being matched by the reduced lateral adhesion of the driving wheels due to the increased driving force transmitted. If the component of the centrifugal force acting in the plane of the rear wheels and the driving force necessary to keep the car going add up to a total at least equal to the adhesion of the rear wheels, there is no adhesion left to hold the wheels laterally and the car just spins out. The value of the optimum drift angle which must obviously exist between the extreme conditions where there is no drift and the one reached when the car spins, is obtained when, for a bend of a given radius, the limit of adhesion of the driving, wheels is reached under the combined action of the lateral component of the centrifugal force and the driving force, this being just sufficient to keep the car moving at the highest speed possible under the prevailing conditions. Up to now, for the sake of simplicity, we have assumed that the forward force put through the driving wheels inevitably reduced the resistance these wheels were able to oppose to forces acting at right angles to their plane, in the first instance the main component of the centrifugal force acting upon the car. This is quite correct, but it does not allow for the fact that any force put through the driving wheels causes a weight transfer from the front to the rear wheels.

Due to this weight transfer, the adhesion of the tire on the road, which is proportional to the weight it carries, is increased, so that in the formula $F_1 = \sqrt{(\text{Total Adhesion})^2 - F_p^2}$ (see Fig. 33), F_1 is not necessarily smaller than the adhesion of the tire under static conditions.

The weight transfer is proportional to the vehicle's acceleration, proportional to the height of the center of gravity and inversely proportional to the wheelbase.

It can be shown that, up to a certain point, and due to the weight transfer, the ability for the rear driving wheels to resist sideway forces is actually increased when a driving force is put through them. If a greater force is transmitted, however, the ability to resist sideways forces is reduced again.

A driver who drifts his car through a bend instinctively finds this optimum condition where the maximum adhesion is available at the rear wheels to combat sideway forces. If, with the car in this condition, the throttle is shut suddenly, the weight transfer is reversed, increasing the load on the front wheels. As at the same moment the lateral component of the driving force acting upon them is also cancelled, they suddenly regain grip; their combined slide and slip angle is reduced to a much lower value than the drift angle at the rear wheels, creating a condition of violent oversteer, which will most likely send the car spinning off the track.

The drift being, within certain limits, a state of equilibrium, it is comparatively easy for a competent driver to keep the car drifting along the desired line. The slight rear-wheel slide that, added to the slip, will put an understeering car at the required yaw angle can only be reached under the combined action of the centrifugal and driving forces. At the moment the car is turned into the curve and centrifugal force builds up, the inertia of the vehicle around its vertical axis, and the driving force which creates a component acting laterally upon the front wheels as soon as they are turned, combine to increase the tendency of the vehicle to understeer. The component of the driving force acting laterally upon the front wheels can be suppressed by releasing the throttle at the precise moment when the car is turned into the curve; the forces resulting from the vehicle's inertia around its vertical axis, however, can only be reduced, but never suppressed, by turning the car progressively into the curve.

This can easily be done when the car is driven into a fast curve, but is difficult when it enters a sharper corner. Here a racing car may show an embarrassing tendency to understeer that can only be counteracted effectively

66

Drifting a Car
Through a Bend

Fig. 42. On slippery ground and dirt roads, the fastest way to corner a rear wheel drive car is to put it in an oversteering attitude and balance it against centrifugal force by a combination of wheel spin and opposite lock.

by turning the car into the corner while the brakes are still being applied moderately. The braking produces a weight transfer from the rear to the front axle, decreasing the former's adhesion in favor of the latter's, and thus encouraging the rear axle to slide out under the influence of the centrifugal force as soon as this reaches a high enough value. At this precise moment, the brakes must be released and the power applied, so as to keep the car drifting round the bend at the highest possible speed. This technique of initiating the drift by keeping the brakes slightly on while the car is turned into the bend calls for extremely precise braking. If the car enters the corner a little too fast, and the brakes have to be applied a little too hard, a spin is almost inevitable; if conversely the speed is a little too low, or if to avoid slowing up the car too much the brakes are not kept applied until the vehicle is turned into the curve, it may be difficult to get the drift started.

The analysis of the forces acting upon a car rounding a bend makes it quite evident that though a front-wheel driven car entering a bend can be balanced to take an appreciable yaw angle, it cannot be kept drifting, except artificially by the use of the hand brake or by having recourse to left foot braking. Due to the driving torque applied to the front wheels and to the weight transfer which occurs under acceleration (decreasing the adhesion of the front wheels), it is inevitable that, if they are called upon to transmit a driving force, they will reach the limit of adhesion first and slide out under the effect of the centrifugal force. This means that the car will understeer and if, by applying more lock or reducing the torque transmitted by the front wheels, the car can, up to a certain point, be kept on the desired line, it can never be pointed in the direction of the exit of the curve before completing it, as does a drifting rear-wheel drive car. This is an inherent disadvantage of a front-wheel drive car as it means that full power for acceleration cannot be applied until the car has completely rounded the bend—that is at a later moment than is the case with a rear-wheel drive car.

This disadvantage of front-wheel drive applies even in the case of small vehicles where the adhesion of the front wheels is adequate to transmit the available power. Front-wheel drive which, due to the reduced front-wheel grip under acceleration, is practical only for cars of moderate power-to-weight ratio, is at an advantage only in sharp corners. In these, the front-wheel lock is such that with rear-wheel drive, the driving force generated at the rear wheels gives rise to a lateral component acting upon the front wheels, which reduces their resistance to sliding more than the driving force that must be applied to the front wheels of an equivalent front-wheel drive car, to get the same acceleration.

67

*Drifting a Car
Through a Bend*

In conclusion, we can say that, due to the yaw angle taken up by a rear-wheel drive car drifting round a corner, the component of the centrifugal force acting at a right angle to the wheel planes is reduced compared to what it would be if the yaw angle were nil, that is if the car cornered in a neutral attitude. Thanks to this, it can be cornered at a higher speed than it would if it remained neutral. As the yaw angle increases, however, so does the component of the centrifugal force acting along the longitudinal axis of the car and opposing its forward motion, until any further increase of the yaw angle causes the vehicle to stop rolling altogether and to slide broadside on to a stop or a crash.

On high grip surfaces, modern high-performance tires do not allow large drift angles to be used, as the grip drops rather sharply as soon as the combined effect of lateral force and driving force break the grip and allow the (rear) driving wheels to spin by a noticeable margin. As we shall see later, large yaw angles also have a detrimental effect on the aerodynamic down force that has helped modern competition cars reach extremely high cornering speeds.

Conditions are very different in the case of the low grip surfaces with which competitors often have to deal in rallies. These usually include a large part of unmade roads or roads covered by snow and ice, examples being the Monte Carlo and Swedish Rallies.

Here the high drift angle technique is the rule and the only means of achieving the best results. Right from the entry into a bend, the driver sets up the car to negociate it in a large four-wheel drift with the car at a considerable angle to the direction of motion, controlling it with both the steering and the accelerator pedal. To achieve the desired drift angle, the driver balances the car before entering the bend by taking a line as described by Fig. 24 (transitory turn), but exaggerating it to achieve a swinging motion and deliberately provoking a slide, going into the bend, usually by lifting the accelerator very shortly to shift weight away from the rear wheels as the car is turned in, and immediately accelerating hard to break the grip.

This method of setting the car up can be achieved even with a front wheel driven car, but requires a special technique. In this case, at the precise moment the tail is required to swing out, the driver must operate the brake pedal while accelerating hard. This will momentarily lock the rear wheels which become unable to resist the centrifugal force and allows the tail to swing out, while the front wheels, even though they are being also braked, continue to rotate because the driving torque applied to them exceeds the braking torque. To facilitate the maneuver, the braking system is usually balanced to provide more rear-wheel braking than is normally the case in front-wheel driven cars.

*Fig. 43. On loose ground or on snow, 4-wheel drive cars can be drifted after hav-
ing been set up for the bend, as long as front and real axles are solidly connected.
This is achieved automatically either by a viscous coupling, a torque-sensitive
center differential, or an electronically controlled clutch locking the central differential as soon as wheel spin sets in. In contrast to rear-wheel drive, the best
results are achieved with smaller drift angles and no opposite lock, because grip
is broken on both axles, as demonstrated by this Audi Quattro.*

The general attitude of a four-wheel drive car is rather similar to that of
front-driven cars, but is dependent on the front/rear torque split. In contrast
to front-driven cars, the drifting attitude can be retained by applying power,
though drift angles tend to be smaller and more power can be applied than
in either rear- or front-driven cars.

Whatever the surface, between cornering within the limits of adhesion
with the car in a more or less neutral attitude and the broadside, there is an
attitude for which the highest possible cornering speed is reached. It is up to
the driver to find thisattitude and to keep the car at the optimum yaw angle
by means of judicious use of the steering wheel and the accelerator. This explains why, in racing, even though a car appears to be cornering perfectly
steadily along a pre-determined line, the driver is usually seen to be moving
the steering wheel to and fro in rapid movements. What he does is merely to
correct incipient slides tending to alter the yaw angle upon which he has settled. They are means to an end, not a means in themselves, as some people
seem to think, who believe that for fast cornering it is essential to impart

Fig. 44. Le Mans is not always easy. Here I come back to the circuit after mis-judging the braking distance under poor weather and visibility conditions. 1st place, however, was not lost in the process.

rapid alternate movements to the steering wheel. On the contrary, the best driver is the one who is able to detect any unwanted movement of the car while it is still so small that it can be rectified by a mere touch of the steering wheel. A real top-rank driver can feel what the car is going to do even before it has started to do it, and act accordingly. Recourse to large movements of the steering wheel to keep the car on its course, is the hallmark of a bad driver.

Aerodynamic Aids

Though, for many years, fashion rather than aerodynamic consider-ations dictated the shape of production cars, racing car designers have been aware of the importance of reducing aerodynamic drag from the beginning of motor racing history. But while the influence of aerodynamics on speed has long been recognized, the influence the air flow had on a car's road be-havior was not generally recognized before the early sixties. True, the rocket powered Opel record car of 1928 had an inverted aircraft wing on either side to make sure it did not take off, but this was hardly a practical proposition. And when that brilliant engineer, the Swiss Michael May who in younger years was a successful racing driver, appeared for the 1955 Nürburgring 1000 Kilometer Race with a Porsche 550 Spyder boasting a large airfoil towering above the cockpit and proceeded to lap faster than the works cars, it seemed so freakish that the scrutineers turned it down!

Most cars are indeed subject to aerodynamic lift, which increases as the square of their speed. This is roughly due to the fact that the way from front to rear along the upper surface is longer than the way along the surface facing the road. Consequently the relative speed of the air flowing over the upper surface is greater than the speed of the air flowing along the surface facing the road. This creates a pressure differential tending to lift the vehicle, following the principle of any airfoil. In single seater cars which traditionally have exposed wheels, additional lift is created by the wide tires, as the air flows over their upper surface at a relative speed double the car's speed, while no air flows underneath the tire.

While the overall reduction of the grip due to lift reduces the cornering and braking potential, the distribution of the low pressure zones on the car's upper surface is at least as important as it governs the variations of the load carried by the front and rear axles as a function of the vehicle's speed. In most modern conventional road cars, specially the closed ones having a sloping bonnet line, the lift reduces the weight bearing on the rear wheels more than on the front wheels, which is exactly what is *not* wanted. This means that the higher the speed, the lesser the grip of the rear wheels compared with the front wheels and consequently the greater the tendency to oversteer. This also goes for racing cars with exposed wheels which are usually much wider at the rear than at the front and consequently produce more rear than front lift.

Considering the case of a rear-wheel driven car, we have seen that, due to the driving force always being applied along the longitudinal axis of the vehicle, understeer increases as the lock of the front wheels is increased. There is consequently less understeer in fast bends than in slow turns. This again is the opposite of what we want. Add this to the aerodynamic forces which further reduce rear wheel grip more than front wheel grip as speed increases, and a car set up to be near neutral in slow corners will be undrivable in fast bends due to high speed oversteer. It is thus very important that the lift, if any, is lower over the rear axle than over the front axle of any car. Without the help of specific aerodynamic devices, this is not easy to achieve in both road and racing cars, specially in conjunction with low drag.

An example of the efficiency of such devices, even in a road car, is given by the pre-1990 model Porsche 911. Without the addition of the front air dam and of the rear "tea tray" spoiler, the total lift force at 150 mph is 180 kg (roughly 400 lb) or 15% of the car's weight, of which 125 kg act on the rear and 55 kg on the front wheels—a distribution which is exactly the contrary of what would be desirable if we allow that we must live with the lift. With the add-on aerodynamic devices, there is still some lift left, but it is reduced to an almost negligible total of 17 kg (37.5 lb), reducing the lift over the rear axle to 12 kg (26.5 lb) and over the front axle to 5 kg (11 lb)—still an undesirable distribution, but in absolute terms, the difference is so small that it can be neglected, and the handling is vastly improved.

In modern racing cars, the body is shaped to achieve down force, both by ground effect and by the use of front and rear airfoils (see Fig. 45). To restrict the effect of these devices to acceptable levels, the bodies governing motor sport have set limits to their dimensions and location.

Nevertheless, centripetal accelerations of over 4.5 g have been obtained in Formula One cars, which means that the centrifugal force acting on the vehicle (and its driver!) is approximately 4.5 *times* its own weight. The down force obtained at 200 mph can exceed 1500 kg (3300 lb) which makes it clear why the suspensions of modern racing cars are so stiff. There is however another reason for their stiffness: the ground effect requires that the ground clearance be kept within very close limits, whatever the load on the car. The incidence of the vehicle (i.e. its angle relative to the road in a side view) is also very important. Even a very small amount of positive incidence (front higher or rear lower than the designed position, or both) can produce considerable front end lift (or dramatically reduce down force) while also dramatically increasing the drag, and there have been cases of racing cars taking off and ending up upside down.

It must also be remembered that airfoils are most efficient when the air flow hits them perpendicularly, i.e. when the car moves in a straight line in still air. When taking fast bends, the deviation is usually not sufficient to seriously reduce their efficiency, but as soon as the yaw angle becomes larger, the down force and consequently the grip are drastically reduced, making the car uncontrollable. This is another reason why large drift angles are incompatible with modern racing cars.

More details on the effects of down force will be found in Appendix 3 at the end of this book.

Chapter V

From Theory to Practice

Setting up the Suspension

Whether a modified road car or a pure racing car is considered, it is essential, if the road surface is reasonably smooth, to reduce any movements of the body which might upset the car's balance, as any departure from the static conditions will modify the position of the wheels and the aerodynamic balance. For example, roll will modify the wheel camber and possibly make the wheels toe in or out, while squat under acceleration will considerably upset the front/rear lift or down force balance. A further general rule is that on a wet road surface, softer suspension and damper settings can be used, as the reduced grip reduces the possible transverse and longitudinal forces (centrifugal, driving and braking forces) to which the car is submitted. The softer suspension and damping allow a more constant contact between the tires and the road and consequently provide a more consistent grip.

To set up a car to handle as the driver requires, the following mechanisms must be understood.

Roll Stiffness

Due to the resilience of the springs and the fact that, as a rule, the center of gravity of the sprung masses lies above the roll axis (the imaginary line joining front and rear roll centers), any lateral force applied to the car will create roll. In this case, we shall consider only the case of a car taking a turn and thus subject to centrifugal force. We will also assume that the roll stiffness is equal front and rear and that the slip angles induced by the centrifugal force are also equal front and rear, resulting in a neutral steering car.

Let us now suppose that we replace the rear springs with solid blocks. In this case there can be no roll and the front springs will remain unaffected, while the entire load transfer caused by the roll torque will be born by the rear axles. As a consequence, the rear slip angle will be considerably increased, while the front slip angle remains unaffected. The result will be a sharply oversteering car. It follows that any increase in rear roll stiffness, whether obtained by increased spring stiffness, raising the roll center or using a stiffer anti-roll bar, will result in more oversteer (or less understeer), while increasing the front roll stiffness will provide more understeer (or less oversteer).

But remember that unless a strong limited slip differential is fitted, increasing the anti-roll bar stiffness on the driving axle is detrimental to traction when cornering as, when the car rolls, the anti-roll bar tends to lift the inside wheel off the ground.

Damper stiffness does not intervene in the ultimate roll angle, but it obviously affects the car's transient behavior, i.e. its response to turning into a bend, as it increases the roll resistance until the ultimate roll angle has been reached. Consequently, stiffer rear shock absorbers momentarily increase the rear roll stiffness, resulting in more initial oversteer (or less initial understeer) and quicker turn-in, while stiffer front dampers will momentarily increase understeer and reduce the responsiveness.

Wheel Camber

We have seen that increased positive camber produces increased slip angles and that, up to a certain point, negative camber reduces them. This provides another way to adjust over- or understeer though, as a rule, positive camber also causes earlier breakaway and reduces possible cornering speeds.

With modern flat treaded and wide racing tires, the limits between which the camber can be adjusted are very close, as any deviation from O° causes unequal load distribution over the width of the tread and may lead to overheating of the overloaded part, causing destruction of the tread. In this case, the best results are obtained by adjusting the camber as well as the tire pressure in such way that after a few laps at racing speeds the temperature is nearly equal over the entire width of the tread. Usually three checks are made with the help of a special gauge: one on the outside of the tread, one in its center and one on the inside. A uniform spread is usually obtained with a very slight negative camber of a few minutes which turns to ± zero on the more important outer wheels when the car is cornering and the wheels lean in unison with the car's roll angle.

Toe-in and Out

Any toe-in or out will obviously increase the rolling resistance and tire wear. Consequently, whenever possible, the wheels should be kept parallel when the car is driven in a straight line. This is particularly important with ultra-wide and grippy racing tires. Slight front wheel toe-in will sharpen the steering response when the car is driven from a straight line into a bend, while toe-out makes the response more progressive. But more important than the toe-in or out itself are the toe variations induced by the suspension movements.

If compressing the front suspension causes the wheels to toe-in (bump toe-in), oversteer is induced as the car is turned into a bend because, as the car rolls, the lock angle of the outside wheel (which carries more load than the inside wheel and thus determines the line take by the car) is increased and the driver must unwind the steering to keep the car on the desired line. Inversely, bump toe-out makes the car less responsive, as roll reduces the lock of the outer (leading) wheel. The former case makes it very difficult to hold the car on a clean line and will also produce a very strong "tuck-in" reaction if the accelerator is lifted in a bend, causing weight to be transferred to the front suspension and consequently increasing the toe-in. The toe variations are mainly dependent on the relative positions of the suspended and non suspended ends of the track rods and can be adjusted by raising or lowering the steering rack (depending on its position) or raising or lowering the position of the ball joint on the steering arms.

Toe variations of the rear wheels are equally important and amount to passive rear wheel steering. Toe-in on bump which causes toe-in of the outside (leading) rear wheel when the car rolls in a bend partly compensates for the slip angle and the car behaves as if the slip angle were smaller than it actually is. It consequently promotes understeer, while toe-out promotes oversteer and makes the car difficult to drive.

While in cars designed for racing the front toe variations can in most cases be easily adjusted, such adjustment is more difficult in production cars, though it is seldom necessary. Rear toe variations are usually dictated by the basic suspension design, though static toe-in adjustment is usually provided in production cars and is the rule in racing cars. Ideally, the rear static toe-in should be adjusted to be as small as possible, but be such that compressing the suspension never produces any toe-out. If—as is the rule in production cars—the suspension links are pivoted on rubber bushings (which for competition work should be as hard a possible or, if legal, replaced with solid bushes or spherical joints), it is desirable to adjust the rear wheels to have sufficient toe-in not to toe-out when transmitting braking forces.

Obviously all considerations regarding rear wheel toe-in can only apply to cars with independent rear suspension. When a beam axle is used, no toe variations or adjustments are possible.

75

Toe-in and Out

Caster Adjustment

The larger the caster angle, the higher the torque calling the front wheels back to the straight ahead position. In racing cars, the caster is readily adjustable to meet the driver's preference. A large caster angle increases the heaviness of the steering, but provides more feedback or "feel."

Weight Distribution

For correct handling, it is essential that the weight carried by the two wheels of one set is equal. Especially with the hard suspension of modern racing cars, this is highly important and must be checked and adjusted on a perfectly flat and level surface. A check that the car is on an even keel is not sufficient, as this can be the case with most of the weight bearing on two diagonally opposed wheels with the other two hardly touching the ground.

Tire and Wheel Sizes

As we have seen before, the wider the wheel rim and the smaller the tire's aspect ratio, the smaller the slip angle under any given conditions. Wider rims also allow the use of larger treaded tires which have a larger contact area also contributing to reducing the slip angle and improving the grip. The use of larger diameter wheels and tires also increase the grip, as they also increase the area of the contact patch. Consequently, whenever possible or allowed by the regulations, larger diameter and wider rear tires on appropriate wider and larger diameter wheels will reduce oversteer when fitted to the rear axle and reduce understeer when used at the front. In the case of driven wheels, they will also improve traction.

Tire size is obviously also a function of the load carried. In most racing cars designed as such, the rear wheels carry a noticeably greater load than the front wheels in order to achieve better traction. They are additionally loaded by the weight transfer under acceleration and, the car's center of gravity being well to the rear, they are submitted to higher cornering forces than the front wheels. This makes it necessary to use noticeably larger tires at the rear than at the front in order to keep the car in proper balance.

Very wide tires are not a panacea however. They increase the air drag, particularly so in uncovered wheel racing cars, but also in road cars or road car derived racing models. They also tend to "tramline" and they start aquaplaning at comparatively low speeds. While for road cars, a compromise must be accepted, for racing and rallying three main types of tires are used, usually called "Dry," "Intermediate" and "Wet." Modern dry tires are "slicks," devoid of any draining groves in order to obtain the best possible lateral rigidity and put the largest possible area of rubber on the road. Their use on public roads is forbidden, as even a very thin layer of water on the road surface makes them very dangerous. Intermediate tires feature enough groves to drain water from the contact area whenever the layer of water on the road surface remains comparatively thin, while wet tires with larger draining channels must be used in a downpour. On a dry surface, both the intermediate and the wet brands—particularly the latter—have less grip than dry slicks and are consequently slower. But the different rubber compound of which they are made and their smaller contact area (where there are groves, there is no rubber) quickly result in overheating as soon as the road dries, which makes the rubber excessively soft and finally results in the destruction of the tread by the centrifugal force acting upon it.

Even among slicks, the tire manufacturers provide a choice of different compounds to meet the requirements of various circuit shapes and surfaces, as well as climatic requirements. In cold weather, softer compounds are used, and it is quite normal practice to fit tires of different compounds to one and the same car. On a clockwise circuit where the left tires are more stressed than the right ones, it often happens that a harder compound is used on the left side wheels and a softer compound on the right side ones. For rallies, completely different brands are available, from slicks which are used only on special stages run on dry, hard roads, to tires suitable for dirt roads, for mud, for snow and for ice, the last two being more or less extensively studded, but even studded slicks are occasionally used!

Springing and Damping

Here too, the requirements of racing on a closed, specially designed circuit and of rallying on closed public roads or on unmade tracks are vastly different. Both single seater racing cars and so-called "racing sports cars" (Group C and similar) rely to a large extent on down force to achieve extremely high cornering speeds. Much of this down force is generated by ground effect, the appropriately shaped bottom of the car acting as a sort of venturi creating a partial vacuum aspirating the vehicle towards the ground. The vacuum generated depends greatly on the distance between the bottom of the vehicle and the road surface. Any deviation from the optimum distance reduces the partial vacuum and consequently reduces the grip the car can oppose to cornering, braking and driving forces. As the down force exerted by the ground effect and the airfoils (which increases as the square of the speed) is applied to the sprung part of the car (regulations forbid direct action on the sprung parts), and can be more than four times the weight of the car (see Appendix 3), very stiff springing must be used—at least until reliable, quick-acting self-levelling devices or active suspensions are devised.

78

Springing and Damping

Fig. 45. Down force generated by ground effect thanks to sophisticated under-body design and by airfoils, of which the dimensions and positions are limited by regulations, can be as high as 3500 lb at 200 mph. Note the multiple adjustment facilities of the "double decker" airfoil of this Formula One Leyton House March.

As a rule, the softest possible springing compatible with the retention of good ground effect efficiency should be used, which implies that, on very fast circuits, where airfoil incidence is reduced and some down force is sacrificed in favour of lower drag, softer springing is used than where the accent is on down force rather than low drag. The softer springing not only ensures a more constant grip between the tires and the road, but also a better interaction between the front and rear suspensions and hence a better response to anti-roll bar adjustments. The damping should be adapted to the springing stiffness and is very important, as when very stiff springs are used a resonance could occur between the tire and wheel springing frequency and the car's own frequency. In view of the very short suspension travels, it is also essential that the dampers respond to the slightest movements. Too soft springing or inadequate dampers can also cause "pumping:" the ground effect pulls the car down and as the ground clearance drops below the optimal value, the ground effect is reduced and the car moves up only to be pulled down again as optimum ground effect is restored.

*Fig. 46. The author testing the Mazda 787 at Paul Ricard Circuit in 1992,
making the best of a fairly wide track, entering a slow (approx. 65 mph) bend.*

Due to the very short suspension travel of modern single seaters (of the
order of 1/2 inch front and 1 inch rear from full bump to full detent), the suspension geometry has become relatively unimportant compared with the
aerodynamic efficiency and tire technology.

In production car racing, stiff suspensions are used mainly to reduce
roll, squat and brake dive, roll being further checked by anti-roll bars which,
as a rule, are adjustable to suit individual tracks and individual driver's pref-
erences. But the suspensions can never be as stiff as in pure racing cars
which, today, are based on immensely stiff carbon fiber monocoques. Touring car bodies, even when reinforced by a specially designed roll-over cage,
are not sufficiently rigid to cope with the inputs of such hard suspensions
without acting themselves as an undamped spring linking the front and rear
suspensions and inducing unwanted resonances.

To sum up the chassis tuning, here is a synopsis of the basic principles:

To reduce oversteer or increase understeer:
• Increase front roll stiffness by using stiffer springs or increasing front
anti-roll bar stiffness and/or ...
• Reduce rear roll resistance by using softer springs or reducing rear
anti-roll bar stiffness. (Remember that increasing the anti-roll bar
stiffness on the driving pair of wheels will result in reduced traction.)
• Use less front negative camber and/or more rear negative camber,
within permissible limits.

• Use narrower front rims and/or wider rear rims, with appropriate tires.
• Use lower front tire and/or higher rear tire pressures, within permissible limits.
• Increase rear wheel toe-in, within practical limits.

To increase oversteer or reduce understeer:
• Invert the above recommendations.

To reduce turn-in abruptness:
• Adjust steering geometry to slightly toe-out when suspension is compressed.
• Adopt slight toe-out in static position.
• Increase front damper stiffness or reduce rear damper stiffness.

Aerodynamic Tuning

All racing cars, including touring cars modified for racing, use aerodynamic devices to produce down force and consequently improve wheel grip. Regulations forbid these to be mobile and consequently they must be adjusted to provide the best compromise between high down force and low drag, as any increase of an airfoil's incidence results in increased drag.

In pure racing cars which make the best of the ground effect, the airfoils are provided to both increase the down force and adjust the front/rear distribution. In contrast, modified production cars usually use a front air dam and a rear airfoil to cancel the lift to which they are usually subjected in standard form, to try to produce some down force and adjust and front/rear distribution of the lift or down forces.

In chapter 4, we have seen that, due to the fact that in a rear-wheel driven car, the driving force is always directed along the longitudinal axis of the vehicle, any such car (the normal configuration of a racing car) will increasingly tend to understeer as the front wheel lock is increased, unless aerodynamic devices are used to counteract this behavior by increasing their grip. Consequently, if a car is set up to slightly understeer in fast bends—an indispensable requirement if the car is to be drivable in such conditions—it will inevitably understeer excessively when taking a tight turn. Thanks to the adjustable aerodynamic aids, this can be largely avoided. For this it is necessary that the aerodynamic devices are adjusted to produce more down force over the rear axle than over the front axle. The chassis can then be adjusted not to understeer excessively in tight turns, and as the down force and consequently the grip will increase as the square of the car's speed more rapidly on the rear axle than on the front axle, the car will understeer more as the speed increases. It will thus remain stable in fast, large radius bends without necessarily displaying excessive understeer in tight turns where the influence of the aerodynamic aids is relatively unimportant compared to the chassis settings. As the contrary is the case in fast bends, the best way to proceed is first to set up the chassis as desired for the slowest parts of the circuit, with the adjustable aerodynamic aids set to have the least possible influence. This being done, the settings of the airfoils and other aerodynamic aids are adjusted to get the best possible handling in the high speed sections of the circuit which, in turn, may require retouching the chassis adjustments.

81

Aerodynamic
Tuning

Chapter VI

Practicing, Qualifying, Racing

Nowadays, the practicing and qualifying procedures in circuit racing are largely standardized. In Europe the sessions extend over two days, each starting with a non-qualifying practice session following, after an interval for adjustments and eventual repairs, by a qualifying session. It is obviously essential that, before he tries to qualify, the driver has made himself perfectly familiar with the circuit. If he is new to it, it is a good policy wherever possible to go round the circuit with a normal touring car for several laps before the first practice session begins, so as to know at least where the corners are, watching out for any likely source of danger, and also taking note of any possible escape area. Some circuits, like the "old" Nürburgring, which is thirteen miles long and boasts some 170 bends and corners, take a lot of learning. It is difficult for a driver new to it to learn the 'Ring during the official pre-race practice; even if it were possible, the mileage involved would completely wear out a racing car. This is the exception rather than the rule, however, and on the usual shorter circuits the time available is normally sufficient for a driver to learn the course perfectly, without straining his car excessively.

As he gets to know the course better, improving his line through the various corners, the driver laps faster and faster. He increases his average speed by taking the bends and corners at a higher speed, which he does by braking progressively later or even deciding that he can take some of the bends without braking at all, or without even lifting his foot from the accelerator. To start with, the driver uses his own judgement to decide where he must brake for a corner, but as soon as he seeks to reduce his braking distance, he starts looking for anything that can serve him as a marker on the roadside, showing the exact point where to apply the brakes. On most circuits the organisers put up signs at 100, 200, and 300 meter intervals at the approach to the various bends, which considerably help the drivers as they seek progressively to reduce their braking distance, and enable them, when they have reached their target, to repeat the performance on every successive lap.

Some corners may involve a problem for a driver new to them. Not all are ideally shaped or regularly banked. Some may have an irregular contour, a decreasing or an increasing radius, or be made up of a succession of two or more bends in the same direction, which are best taken in one single sweep. In such cases, the correct line through the corner does not necessarily bring the car nearest to the inside verge more or less half-way through the bend, and the correct point to aim at is not always easy to find.

If the driver finds he loses times on a particular portion of the circuit because he has failed to find the best line through it, he should not hesitate to follow a more experienced driver through it or, after the end of the first practice session, to inspect it thoroughly on foot in order to understand the exact shape of the road and to try to visualize the line along which it should be negotiated. Once he has decided on the line that should give the best results, he should try to find some landmark, as close as possible to the inside verge, at which to aim his car, to make sure that he keeps to his predeter-

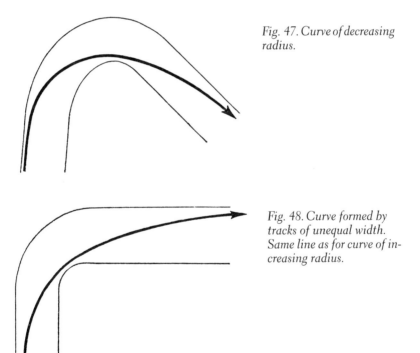

Fig. 47. Curve of decreasing radius.

Fig. 48. Curve formed by tracks of unequal width. Same line as for curve of increasing radius.

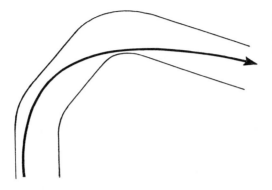

Fig. 49. Irregular curve,
or succession of curves,
to be taken as one only.

84

Practicing

mined line. When practice is resumed, however, he should try his new line
at a comparatively modest speed, to make sure that everything goes according to plan, and then go progressively faster. Never decide to change your
line without trying the new one at a slightly reduced speed first!

Bearing this in mind, the driver will also have found out which gear is
best for any particular section of the circuit. Once he has learned the circuit
well enough to get a good run into its various straights, he can also judge if
the overall gearing of the vehicle is suitable. The lower the gearing, the faster the car will accelerate. The choice of final gear ratio should be governed
by the rpm reached by the engine in top gear on the fastest part of the circuit, when the oil in the engine and transmission have worked up to their
normal temperature. Basically, the ratio is correct if, in top gear, the engine
can reach the highest permissible figure. If this is not attained, it means that
as the gearing is too high, the engine is not able to produce its maximum
power, and not only will acceleration suffer everywhere on the circuit, but
the car will not reach the highest maximum speed of which it is capable on
that particular circuit. On the other hand, if the engine tends to exceed its
maximum permissible revolution rate, the driver will have to lift off the accelerator slightly in order not to damage the engine, or else the engine speed
limiter will intervene and again maximum speed will suffer.

When practicing, doubts may arise as to which gear to use for a specific
bend of the circuit. In one gear, the engine runs near the red line and a shift
into the next higher gear is due as soon as the car has exited the bend, but if
the bend is taken in the next higher gear, the pick-up feels sluggish. In such
case, the best solution is to use the higher gear. One reason is that it will
force you to try to take the bend faster, in order to keep the engine revolu-

tions at a higher level. Another is that any gear shift costs time—no torque is transmitted to the wheels for a fraction of a second. And even if the shift down before the bend has been done while braking, it costs time because it takes some of your attention which should be devoted to entering the bend as fast as possible.

Incidentally, this rule also applies to driving on public roads, be they open to the traffic or closed, as in rallies. Here the exact shape of the road lying ahead in many cases cannot be accurately assessed, and in such circumstances many drivers tend to select the next lower gear, just in case it will be needed. In my opinion, this is wrong, as experience has shown that in at least five out of six cases the shift down was not really necessary. It is undoubtedly better to keep the higher gear engaged, see what happens around the corner, and change down if really necessary as soon as circumstances permit—at latest at the exit of the bend. No doubt, some time will have been lost, but on balance, considering the number of unnecessary shifts saved, this method results in an overall saving of time.

When practice indicates that the gearing must be altered, two cases must be considered. The first is that of a production car modified for racing in which the internal ratios of the gearbox cannot be changed. In this case, the final drive ratio must be changed and all gears will be affected.

This may well mean that more, or sometimes fewer, gear changes will be needed on every lap. If, for example, you had just been able to keep in second gear between two corners without over revving the engine, lowering the gearing will inevitably force you to change up to third for a few yards before you change back again into second for the next corner, and these two extra gear changes may well cost you as much time as you save elsewhere by using the lower gearing. Conversely, you may well decide to use a slightly higher gear just to dispense with the need of changing up for a very short while in a particular case.

In racing gearboxes, all the gears can be changed individually, and optimizing a ratio for any given part of the circuit does not affect the other ratios. In many cases, past experience helps the competitor in the choice of gear ratios for any given circuit, and if no previous experience exists, the more professional teams procure a detailed map of the circuit from which the probable lap time, the speed on any section and hence the required gear ratios can be calculated with the aid of a computer, so that the car arrives on the circuit with a good chance of having the correct gear ratios already installed. But of course, this is only second best to hiring the circuit for one or two days and sorting the car out completely some time before the actual event takes place.

85

Practicing

Fig. 50. Phil Hill's and the late W. von Trips' severely understeering Ferraris follow Brabham's approximately neutral steering Cooper-Climax in the 1960 French Grand Prix at Rheims.

Fig. 51. Jack Brabham again this time performing a perfect piece of cornering in the 1960 Belgian G.P. on the Spa circuit. His Cooper-Climax is held in a copybook four-wheel drift, with the front wheels dead straight, the car being kept in the turn by the fact that perfect throttle control keeps the rear wheels drifting out just a little bit more than the front ones. This is the fastest way of getting around a bend.

In cases where only a small adjustment of the gearing is called for, it can usually be achieved by using a different tire size, though this is applicable to production rather than to specialized racing cars. It must however be remembered that the use of a different tire size may affect the behavior of the car and that small tires reach higher temperatures and wear out faster than larger ones.

On circuits in which a long straight is included, you may want systematically to take advantage of the slipstream of some faster cars, in order to increase the maximum speed of yours. If your car is correctly geared for normal conditions, the speed increase gained by other cars' slipstreams will send the engine revving several hundred rpm above its permissible maximum. To avoid this, a slightly higher gear must be chosen than would normally be used if slipstreaming were not taken into consideration.

The aerodynamic configuration providing the best qualifying time may also not be the best for the race itself. Overtaking—an increasingly difficult maneuver as cars become more evenly matched and braking distances decrease and make it more and more difficult for a driver to outbrake another—can be made easier by reducing the airfoil incidence in favor of a higher maximum speed on straight stretches. The lesser down force will reduce the possible cornering speed, but as overtaking in turns is impossible, this is of secondary importance.

Tires must, of course, be watched with great attention, wear being checked to decide on the policy to be adopted for the race. Soft rubber compounds result in slightly faster lap times, but they wear faster and it must be decided whether to use a harder compound which will last the entire distance, or a softer and faster compound which will require a stop for new tires.

Another very important point to be checked during practice is the fuel consumption which varies according to the circuit on which the race is staged. In long distance racing, this gives an indication as to when the car must be called into the pit for refueling, while in a shorter race, where it is important that the starting weight of the car be as low as possible, it avoids burdening the car with unnecessary fuel.

Qualifying

At the end of the first practice session the car should be at least roughly ready for qualifying. Where qualifying tires are available, their number is usually restricted. These tires have a very soft and sticky compound, providing extremely high grip, but their useful life does not exceed two or, at most, three laps of the current 4 to 6 km circuits, standing start lap from the pit area included. When going out for a couple of qualifying laps, it is thus essential that the driver intensely concentrates on his job and times his departure to get a clear run, as any baulking by another car will ruin his chances. The car must be as light as possible and should only have enough fuel on board to safely complete the qualifying laps. In view of the difficulty to overtake on most of today's circuits, a good qualifying position is extremely important. It also provides the best chances to remain clear of any pile-up that may happen following the start. In Monte Carlo, pole position gives an option of almost 50% on victory.

Even if there are two qualifying sessions on two following days, every effort should be made to get a good qualifying time on the first day, as it may rain on the following day and make it impossible for anyone to improve on the first day's times.

Race Day

It's race day. Even for the most experienced racing driver, it is almost impossible not to feel a bit nervous when an important race lies ahead. If he did not, he could only be accused of lack of interest or lack of imagination. Though the reasons for this nervousness are difficult to analyze, it seems certain that fear caused by the risk involved in every high-speed motoring competition must play an important part. As far as I am concerned, I have always found myself much more nervous before a race in which I stood a good chance of success, than where it was obvious from the start that I would be unable to graduate out of the ranks of the also-rans. This is quite understandable, because when victory seems to be within reach, one is usually prepared to take more risks to secure it, not to mention the greater disappointment that failure will cause. But I have also found that somehow my nervousness could be traced to the fear of making a mess of the start. I always used to be much more nervous before a short race, where a good start is vitally important, than before a long one, and rolling starts are certainly less nerve-racking than massed standing starts. If you drive for a well organized team, the biggest trouble is that there is absolutely nothing you can do to distract your attention from the race before it starts. Your main pre-occupation then is to try and find out if it is going to rain or be fine, whether it is going to be cold or very hot, what sort of tires—fine weather or rain tires—to use, or what your race tactics should be.

Today, drivers have little choice as to what sort of dress they should wear. Even in the hottest weather, modern fire resistant, officially approved overalls and gloves must be worn. Officially approved integral helmets are also the rule and many drivers use multi-layer visors of which layers can be detached and thrown away in case they get blurred by dirt, rain, debris or oil

Fig. 52. Modern racing gear includes compulsory fire-proof over-alls and underwear, both of approved materials, as well as a fire proof head and face cover worn under the helmet, and fire-proof gloves, as worn here by Ayrton Senna.

from preceding cars. In case of rain, an anti-mist compound should be applied to the inside of the visor. If none lies at hand, a trace of soap applied to the inside of the visor and rubbed clear with a dry rag will do the trick as well as most anti-mist compounds. In wet weather, it is also useful to sew a small chamois leather on the back of the gloves to quickly wipe water off the visor, while in hot weather, a bottle of drinking water with an easy to reach pipe should be installed. This is probably possible only in closed cars where more space is available and in which no visor is worn, as this would make the mouth almost inaccessible with the pipe.

The Choice of Tires

In most of the promotion or one-make formulae, the make, type and size of tires to be used is imposed by the regulations and they must be used, whatever the weather conditions.

The higher up the scale we move, the larger the choice of tires. Most manufacturers produce not only dry weather slicks, but also wet weather and intermediate tires, qualifiers, and a choice of different dry-weather slicks (usually three), differing by the compound of their tread. The rule is that the more wear-resistant the compound, the less grip it provides, so that the softest possible compound compatible with tire wear over the race distance should be used. With highly professional teams like Formula One, it may even pay to use the softest possible compound and change tires shortly before half distance. The reason for putting the new tires on *before* half distance is that, at the time of the change, a significant quantity of fuel has been used, reducing the weight of the car, so that the new set will have a lower wear rate.

On circuits featuring more right hand curves than left hand ones (which is the case when a race is run clockwise), it may pay to fit harder tires on the left hand wheels, which are more highly stressed, than on the right hand wheels. In any case, it is highly important to check tire wear during practice, so that the right choice is made before the race. In case of doubt, the tire manufacturer's delegate can usually produce useful advice.

It is, of course important to inflate the tires at the correct pressure. This is usually a matter of experience, but in case of doubt, the car or tire manufacturer can always help. Across the tread temperatures are also an excellent indication: they should be as equal as possible over the entire tread width or if, for the sake of handling, a slight negative camber is used, resulting in a higher temperature on the car side of the tread than on the outside, the temperature in the centre of the tread should be about half-way between in- and outside. A higher temperature in the centre indicates over-inflation; a lower temperature under-inflation.

As the grip of racing compounds for dry surfaces is at its best at temperatures between 75 and 90° C, the top teams use electrically heated covers in which complete wheels are wrapped before use, so that the driver immediately benefits from the best possible grip as he leaves the pit.

Fig. 53. Racing slicks are provided with small holes over the width of the rubber compound. allowing a quick check of tire wear.

91

Choosing Tires

In rallies, racing tires of appropriate dimensions are used whenever the event is run on metalled roads, and in this case too, the competitors have the choice of slicks, rain and intermediate tires. But special tires are provided for the dirt roads over which many special stages are run, while a large variety of snow tires with and without studs, is available for winter rallies. The choice of the right tires in rallies is extremely important and even more difficult than in circuit racing, as the drivers cannot know the exact conditions prevailing in the stage to be tackled. Well-organized teams usually hire an experienced, non-competing rally driver to drive over the stage and telephonically inform the team of the exact conditions, so that the correct choice of tires can be made.

Time Keeping and Communication

During practice, it is essential that the exact number of laps completed by the car and the lap times are accurately recorded to obtain an accurate record of tire wear and fuel consumption. The lap times should be taken for both the team car(s) and the main opponents, so that a target is set to try

Fig. 54. Only approved helmets may be worn. The tube connected to the helmet, worn here by Nigel Mansell, provides oxygen for the driver in case of fire. Some drivers prefer to do without, fearing that the oxygen might activate the fire.

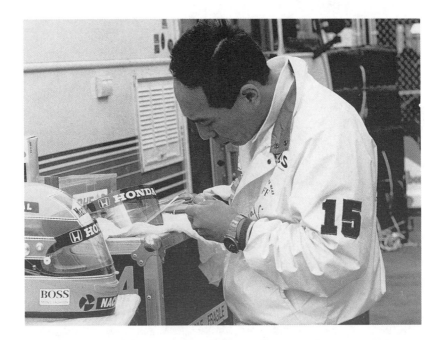

Fig. 55. Good visibility is essential for optimum driver efficiency. A mechanic makes sure that Ayrton Senna is up to his fame.

and get the best possible grid position. Modern electronic chronographs that print out all the times recorded make this a comparatively easy task. All data should be written down on a lap chart on which any adjustment, change of tires or anomaly should be carefully recorded, together with the fuel consumption and such data as tire pressures, oil and water temperature, oil consumption, etc. The influence of the adjustments made on the car's performance and lap times are thus recorded for the final adjustments before the next practice session or the race. Obviously, the driver's comments regarding the adjustments made should also be recorded.

It should not be forgotten that the car may handle differently with full and with nearly empty tanks, so that for the race, the settings should be a compromise, but one favoring full-tank handling, as it is always an advantage to get ahead of as many competitors as possible right from the start and leave any overtaking problems later in the race to them. The fuel consumption having been worked out, the tank should be filled with only the fuel necessary for the race distance (except, of course, in long-distance races), plus a safety margin which should be as small as reasonable, to keep the car as light as possible. In long distance races, the tank must obviously be filled completely, and the fuel consumption calculated after practice will indicate how many laps the car will run on a tankful. To be quite safe however, it is recommended to schedule the first refuelling stop one or two laps earlier to check that under actual racing conditions the consumption is not higher than measured during practice.

During the race itself, in addition to the intervals between the team car(s) and those immediately ahead and behind, it is essential to time every lap of the team car(s). Not only does this enable the pit staff to judge whether the driver can be expected to go appreciably faster or not, it also indicates when the car can be expected past the pits, so that any signals can be shown at the correct moment. This is particularly important during the night hours of a long-distance race, when it is extremely difficult to identify the cars as they approach.

Signalling should be done with figures and letters which are as large as possible, especially when the pit area is situated at a point where the cars reach a very high speed. It is quite a problem for a driver speeding past the pits at perhaps 130 or 140 mph readily to identify his signal, which should therefore be made as recognizable as possible or be given by a person wearing clothing of a bright and easily identifiable color. It is absolutely essential that the signals are given at a point where the driver can devote his attention to them without danger. They must never be given in a zone in which the driver must pick his line for a bend that lies ahead or in a braking area. I once

93

Time Keeping and Communication

crashed a car in practice before a race, because on their own initiative, my pit attendants had elected to give me signals from the pit nearest to their van, which lay just about where I had to start setting the car for the following bend; my attention was retained a little too long by the sign—which brought me off my line—and I could not avoid crashing. Where the pit is badly situated for signalling, you should try to arrange to have another signalling post in a more convenient place. The best spot is the exit from a hairpin bend, before the cars have had time to regain speed.

If he is to go really fast, a racing driver must entirely concentrate on his driving. Therefore the signals must be as simple and readily understandable as possible. For instance, a driver is not interested in the number of laps he has already completed in the race; what he wants to know is the number of laps to go. So if he is driving in a 50-lap race and has just completed for instance his 38th lap, the sign to be shown is not L38, which would force him to calculate himself that he must do another 12 laps, but L12.

The four main items the driver is interested in are:

1) His position
2) His distance to the driver in front
3) His lead on the driver behind
4) The number of laps left to be completed

In some cases, he will also like to know his lap time and to be told of any lap record achieved by himself or another driver. He should also be informed if any of his more dangerous rivals have fallen out of the race.

The first information that should be given is the position. On a short circuit there is no point in giving this information before the various cars have more or less settled down into their respective positions, that is, after the completion of the third or fourth lap. On a long circuit, however, such as the Nürburgring, this information should already be given at the end of the second lap. Subsequently any change in position should be signalled at once because that is what the driver is most interested in. If the car immediately in front of yours has run away enough to be out of sight, the gap between that car and yours should be given for two consecutive laps, so that you can see at what rate you are losing ground. If the pit manager thinks that, on the grounds of your practice times, you could do better than you actually are doing he might put out a sign giving you your actual lap time. The driver knows best under which circumstances he achieved his best practice laps and he will then be able to judge if he can safely go any faster. There is no point in showing lap times if the track is wet, however, as they lack any basis of comparison.

The driver is also interested to know which is the car in front of his. So instead of showing a board reading "-10," which would mean that he is running 10 seconds behind the car in front, the name of the driver handling that car should be added, to read for instance, "-10 Smith." This will help him in his judgement, as previous racing experience or practice will have shown if he can hope to match that particular combination of car and driver or not. If the driver sees that he cannot close the gap between the car in front and his, or if he is out in front of everyone else, he will be more interested in knowing which, and how far, is the next car behind him. Time and again, for instance every five laps, the number of laps left to be run must also be signalled. If, driving as fast as you can, you are closing up at the rate of 1 second a lap on an opponent who has a 30-second lead and there are still 30 laps to go, your race tactics will obviously be very different from what they would be if only 7 or 8 laps were left to be done. With no hope of catching your rival before the end, you would then concentrate on keeping your position while nursing the car as much as possible.

Signalling is quite a difficult task because it is not easy for the person in charge of it to know exactly what the driver wants to know at any given moment. So a code should be decided upon by which the driver can ask his pit for the information he is most likely to want. It may be decided that if the driver points forward with his finger, he wants to know how far ahead is the car in front of him; pointing rearward will then mean, 'By how much am I leading the next man?' Turning circles with his finger may be the code for asking how many laps are left to be run, while tapping with a hand on the helmet is the usual sign for informing the pit staff that the driver intends to come into the pits on the following lap, and everything likely to be needed, such as oil, water, fuel, the jack and the more usual tools, should be kept ready.

Most pit managers usually concentrate so much on their own car and the ones immediately in front and behind, that they tend to forget about the general pattern of the race. Here is an example: your car is running, say, in fourth or fifth position, without being seriously challenged. Suddenly one of the leaders makes a short pit stop and rejoins the race three or four positions behind your car and, say, 45 seconds behind on time. This combination of a fast car and fast driver will now probably start lapping very quickly in an endeavor to make up as many places as possible before the end of the race. A good pit manager will immediately become aware of this menace and signal for instance "+45 Smith;" on the next lap, the signal may become "+42 Smith" and the neat time round "+39 Smith," thus disregarding all the cars that might find themselves between yours and that of the driver who is coming up fast through the field. Having been informed of the danger in time, you may be able to find just that little extra speed that will reduce the average rate at which your dangerous rival is closing the gap from

95

Time Keeping and Communication

96

*Time Keeping
and
Communication*

ASTON MARTIN RACING TIME SHEET.

SHEET No.

EVENT: 1,000 Km. Race   CIRCUIT: Nurburgring   DATE: 1st June, 1958. Sunday,

CAR: CHASSIS NO.: DBR1/3   GEAR BOX NO.:

ENGINE NO.: RB6.300/3   AXLE RATIO: 3.62/1 SH

SPECIAL DETAILS: Red Ident.   No. I   Mechanic - Hones

Circuit length 14.2 miles

DRIVER(S): Moss/Brabham   Gillian Harris

LAP	PLAN	ELAPSED TIME	UNIT LAP TIME	EARLY OR LATE	REMARKS	BAR:	TEMP:	Hg.:
					Hot, sunny		59°F	
1			10-02·4		MOSS SIGNAL 1 LAP	FUEL 130 litres 6.50x16R 6.00x16F	35F/38R	I
2		19-51	9-48·6		SIGNAL +12 MOS, HAW			I
3		29-34·6	9-43·6		SIGNAL +15 MOS, HAW, 3 LAP			I
4		39-17	9-42·4		SIGNAL +21 MOS, HAW (something dragging under car)			I
5		49-06·4	9-49·4		SIGNAL +28 MOS, HAW (light to gearbox bottomed)		+39	I
6		58-58·2	9-51·8		SIGNAL +38 MOS, HAW, 6 LAP		+48	I
7		68-45·4	9-47·2		SIGNAL +38 SAL. OUT		+44	I
8		78-34	9-48·6		SIGNAL +44 LAP 8		+46	I
9		88-18·6	9-44·6		SIGNAL 1 LAP → (4'6" leo) Car sliding, 3rd gear jumping out		+53	I
10		98-08·6	9-50	IN PIT STOP 06·8	Change drivers			I
11		108-42·4	10-27		BRABHAM SIGNAL +41 BRA, HAW (BAW passed pit beyond pit)			I
12		118-59·4	10-17		SIGNAL 1 LAP → (HAW in lead: BRA -37)			2
13		129-21·4	10-22	IN PIT STOP 1-21	Change Driver Fuel (Gearbox OK) Tyres ALL 4 changed ½ gall oil			2
14		140-42	9-59·6		MOSS (←HAW IN)			1
15		150-37	9-55		SIGNAL 1 P MOSS COL		+41	
16		160-35	9-58		SIGNAL +41' MOSS COLL			I
17	(2L 50'27·2')	170-27·2	9-52·2		SIGNAL +52" MOS COL		+1'12·8"	
18	(2L 00:28·2')	180-28·2	10-01	MASTER 3h.00:23·6	SIGNAL +73" MOS, COL LAP 18		+50'	
19		190-17·2	9-49		SIGNAL +80" MOS, COL			
20		200-12	9-54·8		SIGNAL +96' MOS, COL		+1m46"	I
21		210-01·8	9-49·8		SIGNAL +104" MOS, COL		+115"	I
22		219-54	9-52·2		SIGNAL +115" MOS, COL LAP 22		+134"	I
23		229-47	9-53		SIGNAL 1 LAP →		2m31"	
24		239-43·4	9-56·4	IN PIT STOP 07·8	Change Driver Slipping out of 3rd Oil on circuit Oil down to 45 mins gauge			
25		240-27·6	10-36·4		BRABHAM SIGNAL +155" BRA, COL	TEM 70°F		
26		250-47·	10-20·2		SIGNAL +123 BRA, COL		+106"	I
27		261-06·4	10-19·4		SIGNAL +106 BRA, COL		+90"	I
28		271-32·4	10-26		SIGNAL 1 LAP →		+66"	
29		281-07·4	10-35	IN PIT STOP	Change Driver Change tyres Roughly oil 1½ gall FUEL			
30		292-23	1-08 10-07·6		MOSS SIGNAL +71 MOS, HAW		+81	

176.9.44

Fig. 56. Timing chart for the Moss/Brabham Aston Martin DBR1/300 in the
1958 Nürburgring 1,000 kilometres race.

ASTON MARTIN RACING TIME SHEET.   SHEET No. 2

EVENT:.................................... CIRCUIT:.................................... DATE:....................................

CAR: CHASSIS NO.: DBR1/3   GEAR BOX NO.:....................................
ENGINE NO.: RB 6 300/3   AXLE RATIO.:....................................

SPECIAL DETAILS.................................... CAR No.: I

DRIVER(S)....................................

	LAP	PLAN	ELAPSED TIME	UNIT LAP TIME	EARLY OR LATE	REMARKS	BAR:	TEMP:	Hg.:
13	31		302–21·4	9–58·4		SIGNAL +81 MOS, HAW			I
12	32		312–20	9–58·6		SIGNAL +90 O.K		+·99"	I
11	33		322–17·2	9–57·2		SIGNAL +99 HAW, LAP33 (HAW SPUN) +·42"			I
10	34		332–15·6	9–58·4		SIGNAL +262 HAW		+4'1"	I
9	35		342–20·4	10–04·8		SIGNAL +251 HAW		+252"	I
8	36		352–19·4	9–59		SIGNAL +252 HAW LAP36		+4'17"	I
7	37		362–19·4	10–00		SIGNAL +257 HAW, LAP37 Lapped Brooks			I
6	38		372–19·4	10–00		SIGNAL +257 HAW, LAP38			
5	39		382–19·4	10–00		SIGNAL +257 HAW, LAP39			
4	40		392–19·4	10–00		SIGNAL +253 HAW, LAP 40			
3	41		402–23·4	10–04		SIGNAL +250 HAW LAP 41			
2	42		412–31·4	10–08		SIGNAL +243 HAW LAP42			
1	43		422–37·6	10–06·2		SIGNAL 1 LAP			
	44	Th 12m 49·6s	432–49·6	10–12		1st			
						Maxi 6,100			

3 to 2 seconds and thus keep him at bay until the end of the race. If, using less foresight, your pit manager had waited until this faster driver had come up through the field to occupy the position just behind you before warning you of his presence— when he had closed up to say, 10 seconds—it would probably have been too late for you to take any counter-measures.

Though I believe that, in normal circumstances, the pit signals should give the driver information rather than orders, this is a case where the pit manager should take the initiative of putting out a faster sign as soon as he has realised the menace, in order to enable his driver to react immediately. But in the following laps, the signals should make it quite clear why the faster signal has been given.

It is useful for the pit manager to know if the driver has actually understood the signal put out to him. As far as possible all signals which have been understood should be acknowledged by a sign. Signals may be missed by a driver because of bad visibility, or because the signal is hidden by another car which is just being passed. The signalling personnel should be aware of such a possibility and should not hesitate, if necessary, to repeat the signal on the next lap if they believe that it has not been clearly understood. In a long-distance race, it is of particular importance that the signal calling the driver in for refuelling is not missed. Many races have been won by stretching the distance between refueling stops to the utmost, thus saving one stop compared with rival competitors. But this also means that there are only a few drops of fuel left in the tank when the car comes in for refueling and if the driver misses the "come-in" signal, his car is in danger of running out of fuel and being put out of the race. It is therefore a wise precautionary measure to signal the refueling stop twice: two laps before the car is due in, a signal should be put out "In 2 laps;" next time round, the signal should read "In" so that if the driver misses one of the signals, he still knows exactly when to stop.

When night driving is involved, such as at Le Mans, Spa or in the Daytona 24 hour race, it is essential that the signalling panel should be properly illuminated and also be made readily recognizable by a particular color or a large-sized sign attached to it. The normal lighting of the pit area is quite insufficient to enable the driver readily to pick out his own signal from the maze of boards being kept ready to be shown to other cars. It is just as essential that the team car(s) can be easily identified, at night, by the signalling crew, which is usually achieved by arranging one or more low intensity lights of specific colours in a place where they don't disturb the driver but are clearly visible by the pit crew.

99

*Time Keeping
and
Communication*

Fig. 57. The author driving an "Indy" March-Porsche on the occasion of a test drive on the Nurburgring Grand Prix course in 1989.

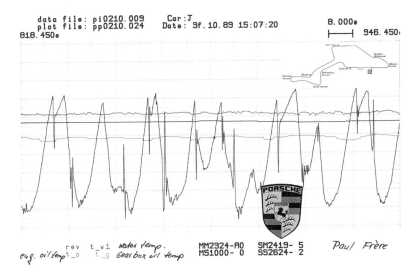

Fig. 58. Portion of a data sheet obtained by telemetry while the author drove the Porsche Indy car. The information provided here are the throttle opening, the boost pressure, the fuel pressure, the oil pressure, and the intake air temperature.

*Fig. 59. Digital instruments have almost become the rule in modern racing
cars. In addition to the tachometer, there is often only one other display board
on which the desired information can be called by the driver as required. In top
flight racing, all the data are displayed in the pit by telemetry and any serious
anomality is brought to the driver's notice, via radio, by the pit personnel. Mi-
crophones are built into the driver's helmet and one of the buttons on the steering wheel establishes contact with the pit at the driver's discretion. The other
button is a safety switch to cut the ignition in the case of an emergency, such
a throttle sticking open.*

Many teams today use radio communication between their cars and
the pit personnel. This can be useful if, for some reason, the driver intends
to make an unscheduled pit stop or seeks a specific information but the initiative of using the system should be left with the driver who will choose an

appropriate moment to communicate, as any interference from outside is bound to affect his concentration, and this could happen at a most inappropriate moment.

Highly professional teams now use very sophisticated telemetry to transmit numerous data directly from the car on the track to the pits where all the major functions of the engine and transmission can be observed and are also stored in a "memory." No driver can cheat any more: any mistake he may make, such as overrevving through shifting down too early (which the limiter cannot prevent) is recorded forever, while the graph also discloses any differences in the driving styles of various drivers.

Race Tactics

The most accomplished racing driver is the one who wins races going as slowly as possible. This principle earned Juan-Manuel Fangio five World Champion titles and Jackie Stewart and Niki Lauda three each—which does not mean that there were not races which they could win only in a brilliant display of their talent.

However, this principle, which the experienced driver should always bear in mind, hardly applies to the newcomer, who will usually have to struggle very hard to get a decent place, rather than win the race with something in hand. Practice times will usually have given you a rough idea of what you may expect from the race. If your practice times indicate that you have a chance of winning it, it may be well worth your while to go as fast as possible and try to challenge your main opponents right from the start, even if this means taxing the engine to its limit and using the brakes to their maximum. By keeping your opponents busy, you may tempt them into overstressing their cars or induce them to make a mistake. Then will be the time to drive to the finish as safely as possible.

On a difficult circuit, a difference in the lap times of two drivers may possibly only reflect the lesser knowledge of the course of one of them who, given more practice, could do better. If it is felt that this may be the case for a potentially dangerous opponent, the obvious thing to do is again to go as fast as possible right from the start so as to build up a useful lead before the opposition, getting a better knowledge of the circuit with every lap, is able to match your speed. This tactic helped me win many touring and sports car races on the Spa circuit, and also to obtain better places in Formula I races than I would probably have managed when matched against the same professional Grand Prix drivers on other tracks.

Unfortunately one does not always have a car that is a match for the opposition but even then, and perhaps more than ever, careful planning may pay dividends. On a fast circuit incorporating long straights, you may decide

101

Race Tactics

to try to "get a tow" from the slipstream of faster cars. This will only succeed if the car you want to follow is not more than eight to ten miles an hour faster than your own. Within this speed range, slipstreaming may push up your speed to lap times which it would be impossible for your car to achieve without outside help. The increase in speed due to slipstreaming will also inevitably result in increased engine revolutions per minute, so that if your car is correctly geared to reach the highest possible maximum speed on the straight when it is driven on its own, the gain in speed due to slipstreaming will bring the revolution limiter into action and your plan will fail, so if you feel that you can rely on "getting a tow" regularly from other cars during the race, it may be useful to gear higher accordingly, as previously mentioned. But bear in mind that the slipstream reduces the efficiency of the aerodynamic devices, which could upset your car's balance in fast bends.

In long-distance races, slipstreaming may be used not to increase the car's maximum speed, but to save the engine and, above all, to reduce fuel consumption. Following a vehicle of equal performance, your car will go as fast as it would go on its own while using about only two-thirds of the maximum throttle opening, and this may enable you to do two or three more laps on a tankful, which may save you one refueling stop in the end.

Even if you are unlucky enough to be driving a car which is completely outclassed, intelligent tactics may bring returns. In a long race, there is always a chance that faster cars will fall out, thus enabling you to get a decent place if your car is driven with this possibility in mind, and treated in such a manner that it stands a good chance of finishing.

If, on the other hand, you know your car to be unreliable, even if it is nursed as much as possible in racing, the better scheme is probably to go as fast as you can for as long as it holds together, in order to put up a decent show while you are in the race. If you do this for a few races, you may hope that someone will notice your performance and offer you a drive in a better car when the occasion arises.

Chapter VII

The Race

T he pit organisation having been laid down, all arrangements having been made for accurate timing and signalling, and the race tactics having been decided upon, you can now concentrate on making a good start.

There are two main types of start: one is the standing (or Grand Prix) start, the other is the rolling start. In both cases, the grid positions are allocated according to the qualification times, the fastest car being "on pole" in the first row.

The Grand Prix Start

In Grand Prix starts, every row is made up of two cars usually staggered by 8 meters in favor of the faster in order to reduce bunching in the first turn following the starting line. Before the start of the race, the cars are sent on a so-called "warm-up" lap in which they must keep their position. This is to ensure as far as possible that all engines are running and to give the drivers a chance to check that everything is in order. At the end of this warm-up lap, the cars stop on their starting position, and as soon as all have come to a full stop, a red light is switched on. From that moment on, the red must turn to green after no less than 4 and no more than 7 seconds, and the race is on. If a driver experiences any problem which might prevent him from making a normal start, he should immediately raise an arm, and the starting procedure is stopped. In that case, the complete starting procedure must be resumed, from the start of the warm-up lap, and the actual race distance is shortened by one lap in order not to upset the fuel consumption previsions of the teams. In minor races, the starting procedure may be different, but the principle remains the same.

To save the clutch release bearing, first gear should be engaged only after the red light is switched on.

In positively deafening noise, at the green light, the clutch should be engaged decisively to avoid burning the linings, engine revolutions being kept up by wheel spin which, in turn, should not be allowed to be excessive for an optimum getaway. In the general cacophony, even the best driver can make a mess of the start, and here good nerves are even more important than expertise.

The Rolling Start

Rolling starts have for a long time been popular in America and are certainly the safest, if not the most spectacular. They are much easier on the clutch, no racing start being needed. The cars are sent on their run-in lap to be covered at moderate speed in the starting grid formation, in some cases behind a pace car, and as they cross the starting line, the flag is dropped and they accelerate away.

In the general confusion and shattering noise of the start, it is difficult to hear one's own engine and also to observe the revolution counter, and it is very easy to over-rev the engine, with disastrous results, unless it is fitted with a revolution limiter; today, this is mostly the case.

Passing

Apart from trying to save split seconds everywhere he can, of which enough has been said in previous chapters, one of the driver's main problems during the race will have to be faced when other competitors must be passed or when a faster car comes up behind.

When two cars and drivers are very nearly equally matched, and are racing neck and neck, there is, of course, no question of the one in front giving way to the other, but it is the duty of the leader to make room for his follower to pass, if he can, whenever it does not bring him off his proper line. For the follower, the only chances to get by his rival are to out-brake him into a corner, to pass him after the corner if he has managed to take the latter a little faster, or by slipstreaming on a straight.

Outbraking is possible only coming up to a slow corner, where the braking area is long enough for the passing maneuver to be performed, but with the incredibly short braking distances of modern racing cars benefiting from heavy down force, carbon brake discs and modern racing tire technology, braking areas have become increasingly shorter and "outbraking" more and more difficult.

To pass exiting a bend implies that the car to be passed is slower through the bend. Having followed a competitor for a few laps, the driver who wants to pass his rival will have observed where the rival is slower than he would be and baulks him. If he continues to follow him closely, he will be baulked on every lap and will be unable to pass. Therefore, coming up to that particular corner, he should allow his rival to take a lead corresponding

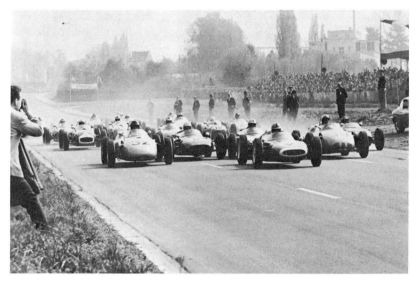

Fig. 60. The cars have just moved away from a massed start, where they were lined up in groups of three, two, etc. Already the cars from the second row have drawn almost level with those which started from the first.

Fig. 61. This is what can easily happen if a driver is too keen to get off to a good start, or if a car fails to move at the fall of the flag. The drivers involved are the late Ron Flockhart jumping Jack Lewis' Cooper just after the start of the 1960 Brussels G.P. for Formula 2.

Fig. 62. *Drivers running to their cars for a Le Mans start. As not all drivers and cars get off to an equally good start, this is a good way of partly sorting them out before they reach the first corner but, if the race is of short duration. This type of start has been abandoned to allow the drivers time to fasten the safety harness. (Le Mans circuit, Tour de France 1960.)*

Fig. 63. *Phil Hill signalling to Trevor Taylor that he is making room for him to pass on his left-hand side. This implies that, if necessary, he will also slow down to make his opponent's task easier. The negative camber used on all wheels of racing cars of the period can clearly be seen in this picture. (1961 Dutch G.P., Zandvoort.)*

to the distance he reckons he could gain by taking the bend at his own, higher speed. This will prevent him from being baulked and, having negotiated the bend faster, he will leave it at a higher speed and easily pass the other car before it has picked up enough speed to match his.

The third method of passing is—as has been hinted before—slipstreaming. An area of reduced air pressure is produced behind any car that is being driven at high speed; this reduced pressure will lessen the air drag of a car that is being driven close behind, thus increasing its speed. Slower cars can take advantage of this to "get a tow" from faster cars, and in the case of two cars of identical maximum speed following each other, the second one will quickly close up on the first, thanks to the reduced air resistance. If its driver pulls out at the last possible moment, he will be able to pass the first car before air drag reduces his speed to its normal maximum. It must however be remembered that in another car's slipstream, the efficiency of the aerodynamic aids is considerably reduced, which can upset the balance of the car.

The drivers involved in a struggle of this sort always use their mirrors extensively to watch their opponent and know exactly what he is about to do. It is therefore current practice and perfectly safe for the car behind to try to pass on either side, whichever is the more convenient and safe.

The problem is quite different when the speed differential of the two cars is greater or the drivers are less evenly matched. A driver who knows that he cannot match some of the other competitors in the race—and he should know from experience or practice times—should keep an eye on his mirrors every time a long enough straight between two corners provides the opportunity of doing so, and occasionally cast a quick glance over his shoulder at a hairpin (if there is one on the circuit), the better to judge the distance between himself and the cars that may come up behind. A faster car or driver should never be baulked by one who is definitely slower, and a driver who does not bear this in mind is bound to make himself unpopular very soon.

As soon as a faster car has come up sufficiently close to be expected to pass at the first opportunity, you should give way to enable it to pass as easily as possible, even at the cost of a few fractions of a second if you are not terribly pressed yourself. For instance, if the faster driver is coming up just behind at the approach to a corner, you should start slowing down a little earlier than usual, yield the better approach position to the corner, and make it quite clear that you are prepared to let the other car pass you, eventually signalling the other driver on which side you are going to make room for him.

There is, of course, no point in losing time unnecessarily, and if you see that you can take the bend without getting in the other driver's way you should do so, and make room at the exit of the curve. If it is a right-hand corner which, following the normal line, you will leave close to the left-hand side of the road, you should stay there and signal the driver behind to pass on the right, and you must not cut across his path again before he can do so.

In races in which cars of vastly different performance run together, as is usual in sports or G.T. car events, passing can become a major hazard. Down the long straight at Le Mans, for instance, the speed differential between the fastest and the slowest cars may be as much as 60 or 70 mph, and if one of the slower cars pulls out for passing when one of the faster cars comes up behind at full speed, a nasty situation may arise. In this case, the driver of the slower car about to pull out is in a better position to judge the speed of the vehicle coming up behind him, than the driver of the faster vehicle is to judge the relative speed of the two slower cars. This is why the driver of a comparatively slow car, who is about to pull out for passing—or maybe only to take his correct line through a corner—should be particularly careful and make quite sure that in doing so he does not cut across the line of a much faster vehicle coming up behind. In any case, the driver of the faster car will be extremely grateful for any signal by the driver of the slower car that will inform him of his intentions. If the slower car is closed, and hand signals are not practicable, the driver may use his direction indicators to show that he is aware of the car coming up, for example by flashing his right-hand side indicators, to indicate his intention to stay on the right-hand side of the road or vice versa.

Flag Marshals

Unfortunately not every driver is a perfect gentleman who is prepared to give way to a fellow-competitor as soon as he is obviously in a position to pass him. Cases of deliberate baulking are fortunately rather rare; they occur more often in second-rate events in which some drivers take part who have no other means of keeping their opponents at bay. Other inferior drivers are kept so busy by holding their car on the road that they don't seem to have any time left for looking in their mirror.

It is for those who never take a look behind that flag marshals, posted along the circuit, have been provided with a blue flag.

When it is held still, it just draws the attention of the driver who gets it to the fact that he is being followed by another competitor who may wish to pass him. If the marshal waves the blue flag, the driver is instructed to make room for a faster competitor who is about to pass him. A driver who feels that he is being baulked by another competitor may appeal to a flag marshal to use his blue flag by waving his hand to draw his attention to the situation.

The use of the blue flag is a much more difficult task than one might

Fig. 64. However quickly the author managed to jump out of his Ferrari for the last pit stop before driving on to win the 1960 Le Mans race, a mechanic has already opened the tank filler cap and is just about to push in the nozzle of the pressurized refuelling system.

think. If the flag is abused, it loses all significance, and drivers cease to take any notice of it. But it must be used when circumstances call for it, otherwise it is just as well to have no flag marshals at all. It is quite difficult for anyone without racing experience to judge when the flag should be given, and when not. A red car is not necessarily faster than the others, and a good flag marshal should not only be fully aware of what is happening in the race, in order to be prepared to show the blue flag at the appropriate moment, but he should also know at first glance who is who and which, of two cars racing in close company, is likely to be the faster one.

Marshals also have other flags at their disposal. Among the most important are:

- The yellow caution flag, used when an incident or accident has happened, requiring special caution and reduced speed. The flag is waved for a time corresponding to two laps and is later held immobile for another two laps—or longer if work is still proceeding on the track—and then removed in order not to create confusion in case another incident should happen in the same area. Once the danger area is cleared, the green flag is shown. *Very important is that any passing in the yellow flag area is forbidden.*

Fig. 65. Every second lost in the pits must be made up by the driver on the road, at great risk to himself and his car. Attention to details can often save precious seconds. Here a mechanic uses a huge syringe to force oil into the reservoir of the dry sump lubrication system of the DB3S Aston Martin, which the late Peter Collins and the author drove into second place in the tragic 1955 Le Mans 24 Hours Race.

- The red and yellow striped flag, used to indicate a zone of reduced grip—usually because oil has been spilled on the road surface, but it can also be used to warn drivers of a local rain shower.
- The white flag indicating that a car is driven at low speed on the circuit.

Only the clerk of the course may use the following flags:

- The chequered flag signalling the end of the race.
- The red flag calling for an immediate stop of racing and drive slowly back to the pit area.
- The black flag shown together with a white number on a black board, which requires an immediate stop at the pits from the car of which the number appears on the board.

Chapter VIII

Speed and Safety

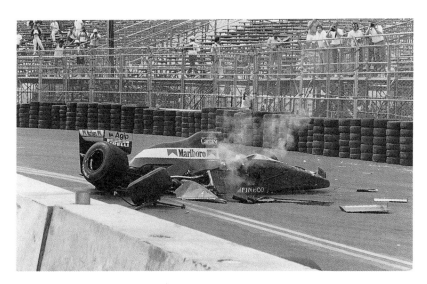

A t speeds of around 180 miles per hour, which is well below the maximum speed of many racing cars, a car travels about 250 feet in every second, needs about 1000 feet to stop, and will travel 50 feet in 1/5th of a second, i.e. in the normal reaction time of a well-trained driver. This means that if anything unforeseen were to happen, the car could easily have left the road before the driver was able to take any action whatsoever. High speeds can thus only be indulged in safely if the driver uses adequate foresight.

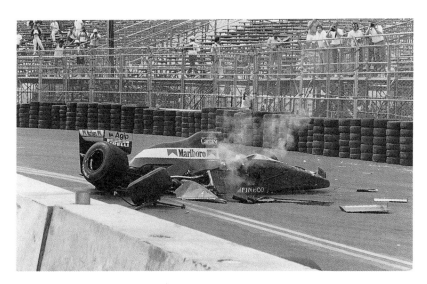

Fig. 66. Modern carbon fiber monocoques: the well-protected location of the flexible fuel tank bladder behind the driver and the combination of roll-over bars and a six-point safety harness make today's single seater racing cars very safe. The driver of this Dallara escaped unhurt from this practice accident.

Circuit drivers who have an intimate knowledge of the course they drive on, and know that it is most unlikely for them to find any obstacle in their way other than rival racing cars, running at approximately the same speed as theirs, do not look nearly as far ahead as they would if they were driving at the same speed on the open road. All the time their mind is devoted to placing the car correctly for the hazard they are about to negotiate, but all the same they must keep an eye on the other cars and watch out for any situation that might lead to an incident, or perhaps an accident, in which they might become involved. The ability to anticipate, not the reaction time, is what matters most in the making of a safe, fast driver. Not only must he know how his own car is to react in any given circumstance—perhaps it is going to start a skid—and take corrective action even before it has begun to do so, but he must be able to observe, for instance, that the man in front has gone into a corner a little too fast, or has come off his normal line, and be prepared for the result, trying to figure out for himself in a fraction of a second, what the other car is going to do—maybe in which direction it is going to shoot off and how he could best avoid it.

Only a highly developed sense of anticipation has kept Fangio out of trouble where other drivers were involved in multiple crashes. One of these happened at Monza in the 1953 Italian Grand Prix when Ascari and Farina were leading him to the finishing line on the last lap when they were brought off their line by another driver and both crashed. Fangio, who was racing just behind, immediately weighed up the situation and was able to avoid both the crashing cars and win the race. Another example is the disastrous Le Mans race of 1955 when Levegh's Mercedes crashed from behind into Macklin's Austin-Healey and killed 85 spectators; Fangio was coming up just behind and was able to drive through the mêlée to safety. A third instance is the multiple crash in the Monte Carlo Grand Prix of 1957 when, on the second lap, with all cars still bunched together, Moss, who was in the lead crashed into a barrier and Hawthorn and Collins, who were following close behind, were unable to avoid being involved in the accident. Even though the road was getting more and more blocked as the cars piled up one after the other, Fangio, who was close behind, again managed to steer his Maserati clear and to victory.

Important as anticipation may be on a track, it is much more so, indeed it is vital, on the less known or unknown roads with which rally drivers and all drivers seeking to go fast on public roads must cope. It is here that the so-called road sense comes in. This may best be described as the faculty for a driver to have his attention attracted immediately by anything that might lead to a change of situation, calling for action to be taken in order to save time, or in the interest of his own or other road users' safety. An experienced driver is very seldom forced to take emergency action; for him emergencies practically never arise.

There is no substitute for experience, but a receptive mind can collect a lot of experience in a comparatively short time and will soon learn where to look out for danger. You cannot look everywhere at the same time, so your eyes and your mind must dismiss at once, and forget, anything that is not of immediate interest, in order better to concentrate on more important things. The ability to distinguish immediately between what is important and what is not can be trained to the point where, out of two dozen people walking or standing on the pavement, you will be able immediately to pick out the one person who is going to cross in front of your car. Many people would be surprised if they knew how much can sometimes be deduced from how little. For instance, a long shadow may herald the approach of a car at crossroads before the actual car can be seen; the fraction of a second that elapses between the moment where the shadow appears and the car can actually be seen may spell the difference between a safe stop and a crash. If, on the other hand, you see pedestrians calmly walking across a crossroad, you may safely assume that no vehicle is about to appear. And if they suddenly jump for their lives, you certainly can draw your own conclusions! In town, shop windows may also reflect a vehicle before you can actually see it—and they can also be very useful when it comes to parking a car in a confined space between two other vehicles.

A car may be stopped on the roadside; your first glance must be for its interior. If it is occupied, people may open a door and step out on to the road; if the driver is at the wheel, the car may start or even make a U-turn. If it is a truck, it may hide a person whose legs you can probably see if you look under the vehicle.

What is important is to know where to look, when to look and what to look for. In town, when another car preceding yours makes a crash stop, compelling you to use your brakes very hard yourself, your reflex should be not to stand on the brake pedal and push it as hard as you can, but rather to use your brakes as smoothly as conditions permit and stop as near the car in front as possible, in order to give the car behind a chance to stop without crashing into your car. As soon as you know you have matters under control, give a glance in the driving mirror to see what is happening behind; maybe it will warrant pulling out to the right or left, if there is room to do so, so that the driver following you gets a chance to cope with the situation.

On increasingly crowded roads, an ever larger number of accidents take the form of multiple collisions of cars being driven in a queue and bumping one into the other when for some reason one of them is brought to a quick stop. Even if you keep a reasonable distance between your car and the one in

113

Anticipation

front, it is absolutely impossible for you to stop in time to avoid hitting it if its normal braking distance is shortened by crashing into another car! This is no excuse, however; a driver must be prepared for that sort of foreseeable incident to happen. Instead of watching only the car ahead of him, he must try to see the vehicle running two or three positions in front so that action can be taken early enough to avoid that sort of crash. In this position he will also have the advantage of occupying a position slightly offset in relation to the car in front, which will facilitate an emergency manoeuvre if it is called for.

Fast but blind motorway bends are taken at speed much more safely if the car is driven in a lane on the outer side of the turn, rather than hugging the inside, as from an outer lane any obstacle ahead can be seen at a much longer distance. And quite logically, as slippery roads increase the stopping distance from any given speed, they require more foresight. On snow, for instance, it is necessary to look about three times as far ahead as one would on dry tarmac.

You may ask what these examples of anticipation, which increase driving safety and are a basic requirement for any good driver, have to do with competition driving. True, not all of them apply to track racing, but rally drivers are faced with all the hazards of normal traffic, and the slightest incident will inevitably mean the loss of much valuable time, not to mention that a competitor in a sporting event will inevitably draw suspicion upon himself, even if this is entirely unjustified. In most of these cases, safety also goes hand-in-hand with speed.

The Emergency Line

Under racing or rallying conditions, circumstances may often make it impossible strictly to apply the rules dictated by theory. Other competitors must be considered, faster cars may pass or slower cars must be passed, which may bring you momentarily off the ideal line. In this case, especially on closed circuits, those parts of the road surface away from the line generally taken by the cars are likely to provide much less grip than those over which the cars are normally driven. This is because they are usually very dusty and full of rubber from the abrasion of the soft racing tyres.

When a driver gets really pressed, one way for him to save split seconds is to leave his braking before a corner as late as possible. Under such circumstances, it is almost inevitable that, on some occasion, he will make a slight error of judgement and leave his braking fractionally too late. If the driver nevertheless persists in taking his normal line, the car will come into the corner too fast and will most probably go off the road or spin. The only way for the driver to extricate himself from this difficult situation is to aim the car at the inside of the curve as soon as he realises that he will not be able to slow the car sufficiently to take the bend in the normal way. In this way the car can be kept on a more or less straight line for a slightly longer distance and the brakes can be kept fully applied for a longer time before the car is turned into the corner. This line will result in a sharper curve round the corner which will thus have to be taken at a slower speed, but at least the worst will have been avoided.

A similar approach to the bend can be made systematically in order to postpone the braking point, compared with the normal line into the turn. As this line deviates from the theoretically fastest line, it implies that the bend is taken at a slightly slower speed, but this is partly or wholly compensated for by the later braking. This line has the further advantage that the braking takes place at a distance from the road side, which is safer, should, for some reason, the car swerve, and it also makes it impossible for another competitor to sneak into the inside in an attempt to pass.

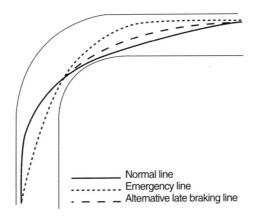

Normal line
Emergency line
Alternative late braking line

Fig. 67. Different lines through a corner.

Driving in Rain

Most ordinary drivers are scared of driving on wet roads. It is, however, mostly a question of adaptation, especially in racing where unforeseen obstacles are fewer than on the roads. In racing, when cornering, braking and accelerating, a car is always being driven at the limit of its adhesion. If this is altered by a wet or damp road surface, the driver's judgement will have to be adjusted accordingly. This means that cornering speeds will have to be lower and braking distances increased, while the accelerator and brake pedals must be treated with more delicacy to avoid locking or spinning the wheels, of which the latter will reduce the car's acceleration and produce unwanted power slides of the tail. On the normal kind of circuit, it will even be found that rain does not change the position of braking points before corners as much as would be expected. The reason for this is that, cornering speeds being lower in the wet, cars leave the corners at a slower speed, which slows them all along the following straight, so that they do not reach the next braking area at the same high speed as in the dry. On a slippery road, any unwanted movement of the vehicle, any incipient slide, must be checked with even greater accuracy and rapidity than usual if it is to be controlled at all.

As, basically, the degree of slipperiness does not alter the driving technique, it makes very little difference how slippery the road is and whether it is made slippery by water, snow or ice. Fortunately the speeds at which bends and corners can be taken become progressively lower as the road gets more slippery, so that everything happens with the car travelling more slowly. As the road gets more slippery, the difficulty shifts from the curves to the straights. Here almost the same high speeds are reached as when the road is dry; whereas in curves the speed of the car must be reduced to lessen the forces acting upon the vehicle so that the balance between these forces and the grip of the tires on the road is maintained. On the straights, only the grip is reduced but not the momentum of the car and the various forces generated by it. On a very slippery surface, such as snow or ice, the point can even be reached where the drag caused by the air and rolling resistance becomes equal to the tractive force of the driving wheels. This sets a limit to the speed that can be reached by the vehicle under the prevailing conditions. At this speed the entire adhesion of the driving wheels is used for propelling the car; the wheels tend to spin and are unable to oppose any resistance to lateral forces that may act upon the vehicle. The latter thus becomes directionally unstable and can only stay on the road if the driver constantly corrects its direction of progress. In practice, this only happens if inappropriate tires are fitted. With winter tires, studded if necessary, such a situation never arises.

Braking distances are of course increased on slippery roads, making it necessary for the driver to look farther ahead for any possible obstruction. This is important enough on the race track, but it is absolutely vital on the open road, where the sight must be concentrated much further ahead—looking out for a bad corner, for a dangerous crossroad, for oncoming traffic when passing or for the odd cyclist. Accurate assessment of how far ahead the eyes must look for any possible danger, in relation to the grip afforded by the road surface, becomes increasingly difficult as the speed rises and calls for considerable experience. Drivers are usually reluctant to look far enough ahead, because the farther they look, the more their attention is distracted

116

Driving in Rain

Fig. 68. Rain does not call for a basically different driving technique. The only difference is that grip is reduced, calling for more delicacy when accelerating and braking, reduced cornering speeds and care to avoid pools of water likely to cause aquaplaning. The by far biggest problem is the lack of visibility caused by the sprays raised by preceding cars.

Fig. 69. In tight turns, 4-wheel drive cars tend to understeer, as does Marc Duez's Toyota Celica 4WD.

from placing the vehicle correctly in relation to its immediate surroundings.

A very heavy downpour, however, may completely change the driving conditions at high speed and make them extremely dangerous. This happens when the rain comes down at a higher rate than the water is drained from the road surface. The road then becomes coated with a layer of water of measurable thickness; at normal speeds, this water is squished away by the tire as it rolls along, and what is not deflected to either side of the tire, finds its way into the grooves of the tread pattern. As the speed increases, however, there is less and less time for the water to escape from under the tire and a point can be reached where not all the water is squished away in time for the tire to make contact with the road surface: it becomes buoyant; the car just floats on the water and becomes uncontrollable. The car "aquaplanes." In such an event there is very little to do, and even the best of drivers can hope that the wheels will reach a patch of road where they can regain their grip before it is too late. Such a situation is more likely to present itself on the modern sort of flat and beautifully smooth road surface, on which the water tends to lie, than on a rougher surface.

It is sometimes said that there are drivers who like racing in rain. This is yet another example of nonsense being talked about motor racing. No driver actually likes, or ever did like, racing in rain, if only because the spray raised by the cars ahead reduce the visibility to virtually nil and makes racing very dangerous—more guesswork than technique. This is bad enough in closed cars, but in single seaters with uncovered wheels and ultra wide tires, the situation becomes catastrophic, with the additional hazard of the visor possible misting up.

No driver therefore likes to race in rain. It is true however that drivers sometimes hope for rain because it will give them a better chance. The more delicate touch that is necessary to get the best results on a slippery track may sort out drivers who on a dry road would be equally matched. Rain can also be an advantage for the car rather than for the driver. Fast and powerful cars are always more handicapped by rain than small cars, as an example will show. Imagine a curve that can be taken at about 130 mph on a dry road; in rain the speed will have to be reduced to say 110 mph, so that all fast cars will be slowed down by 20 mph through this curve. A smaller car, which has not enough power to reach more than 100 mph at this point will, however, not be slowed by the more slippery condition of the road at all; it will take this curve at around 100 mph, whatever the weather and still with a useful safety margin. Rain thus levels out the usable power—which is why the drivers of less powerful cars often wish for rain, even if they don't actually like it.

Winter Driving

There is actually very little difference between driving on a road made slippery by rain and on a road made slippery by snow or ice. Very fortunately, however, racing cars are not as a rule driven over snow-covered or icy roads, where their very high power-to-weight ratio and the lack of flexibility of their engines would make them very difficult to drive, though rally drivers are often faced with such road conditions.

Modern international rallies are decided by the addition of times taken on special stages of which the length can reach from a couple to up to 30 miles. They are linked by untimed sections on which the normal rules of the road must be observed, but which must be covered in a maximum allowed time in order both not to upset the time schedule of the event and to prevent the competitors from undertaking major repairs. Time penalties are assessed in cases when the time allowance is exceeded.

The technique of competitive driving required on snowbound roads is very similar to the technique required on unmade roads, but the choice of tires is very difficult, as the optimal compounds are different for different sorts of snow (wet or dry, loose or hard) and icy stretches require studded tires. Another problem is that on comparatively long timed sections, conditions often differ along the section. This is most likely to be the case in mountain sections where the road can be dry or wet at the beginning of the section and change to snow or ice or both as the road rises into the mountain. Private entrants must perforce make do with whatever equipment they have or manage to have ready in the service area before the start of the section, but top teams can rely on their own or their tire manufacturer's organization to provide the most suitable brand. Their problem is that the drivers have not had a chance to see the section for several days. Meanwhile the conditions can have changed drastically and they cannot decide for themselves which tyres to adopt. This is why top teams hire experienced drivers to go over the section as late as possible before the start and report by telephone on the road conditions, after which a decision about the tires to be used is taken.

Whereas on dry asphalt, four-wheel drive is hardly an advantage over two-wheel drive, the grip advantage of the four-wheel driven models being compensated by higher weight, four-wheel drive is an overwhelming advantage on snow and ice. Four-wheel drive cars tend to understeer and require a special driving technique, rather similar to front-wheel drive. Their behavior is graphically explained in Appendix II. To get the full benefit of four-wheel drive and handling close to that of a rear-wheel driven car on loose or slippery surfaces, most four-wheel drive rally cars use an unequal torque split in which the higher torque is directed to the rear wheels, themselves driven through a limited slip differential. In this context, it must be said that most front-wheel driven rally cars also use a limited slip differential, the limiting device being usually a viscous coupling which works so progressively that it is hardly perceived by the driver.

Racing at Night

Twelve and 24 hours races as well as many international rallies involve night driving. Darkness being an additional hazard, every measure to improve the drivers' comfort should be taken in order to distract him as little as possible from his or her primary task: drive as fast as possible. Disturbances by any bright light, or reflection, from other cars running behind or from your own, should be avoided.

This means that the whole dash, especially the horizontal part at the base of the windscreen, must be painted dull black and so should the instrument bezels, and steering column, the steering-wheel spokes, the rear-view mirror frame and any bright part, particularly if the car is an open one. In this case, the dull paint will also prevent the reflection of the sun during the bright hours, which can become very tiring for a driver whose nerves have already been strained by several hours of racing or rallying. The absence of reflections in the screen is also a great help in fog.

Even in daylight, it is not an easy task accurately to read the figures on the smaller instruments, such as the oil pressure gauge and the oil and water thermometers. For racing, I always made a habit of (a) identifying them by large, white writing painted on the panel itself, such as WATER, OIL.P. and OIL.T., etc., and (b) painting a red line on the glass of the dial in the position approximately corresponding to the normal position of the finger of the instrument. In this way, a mere glance is sufficient to make sure, even at night, that everything is normal.

With this arrangement, it is no longer necessary to have the instruments brightly illuminated: they cause less distraction and a better vision of the road is obtained. The all-vital rev-counter is always large enough not to cause difficulty. Incidentally, when a speedometer is also fitted in addition to the rev-counter, it is a good precaution to mark on its glass the speeds corresponding to the highest permissible engine revolutions in the various gears. This may be useful in case of a rev-counter failure—a not infrequent occurrence.

In my experience, perfect visibility is vitally important if fractions of a second are to be saved: driving a D-type Jaguar in a practice session at Silverstone, changing the slightly scratched goggles I had been wearing for a pair of perfect ones immediately cut down my lap times by 2 to 3 seconds.

If the least possible time is to be lost during the night hours of a race, or on difficult night sections of a rally, the car must have very powerful lighting equipment. For racing, a pair of powerful long-range headlights should be supplemented by two wide-beam fog lights which are not of much use in fog, at racing speeds, but are a great help in illuminating the sides of the road to enable the driver to place his car correctly on bends. For racing, those auxiliary lights are perhaps even more important than the headlights themselves, as, on a circuit, the driver always knows exactly what lies ahead, but for rallying, powerful lights are vitally important.

When coming up behind another car, the lights should be dipped, and an anti-glare, two-position driving mirror is most desirable. The dip switch should be very easy to reach and to operate, and it is a good scheme to have it combined with a device enabling the driver to flash the headlights to warn slower cars before they are passed.

Six powerful front lights, plus all the auxiliaries including, in rally cars, intercom between driver and navigator and a good reading lamp for the latter use a lot of wattage and it is essential to make sure that the car's standard alternator is powerful enough to keep the battery charged with all those consumers switched on.

Less Braking—More Speed

If you want to go fast, keep off the brakes! I will never forget a scene I witnessed at Spa during practice for the Belgian Grand Prix of 1953. The Maserati factory had entered four cars—three for the regular team of Fangio, Gonzalez and Bonetto, and a fourth car for the former Belgian champion, the late Johnny Claes. Try as he might, Claes could not nearly match the times of Fangio and Gonzalez. After much fruitless hard trying, Claes who was a close friend of Fangio's, approached him and asked him if he would try his car because he thought it was slower than the others. Fangio immediately agreed; he jumped into Claes's car and did three or four laps, the fastest of which was almost as fast as he had done in his own car. When Fangio came back into the pits, Claes shrugged his shoulders and said, "But tell me, how on earth do you do it?" Fangio said nothing at first and extricated himself from the cockpit; he then went quietly to sit on the pit counter, with Claes following him and, in his broken English and grinning broadly, gave his very plain and simple explanation: "Less brakes," he said, "and more accelerator."

The assertion that speed is increased as less use is made of the brakes is, of course, a fallacy. To go fast, the brakes must be used, and used very hard indeed, but only where it is essential to slow the car down. For obvious reasons, much more unnecessary use is made of the brakes on the road than on a circuit which the driver knows perfectly. On the road any driver has a strong instinctive tendency to use his brakes as soon as he is not absolutely sure of what lies ahead. More concentration and better observation of any signs which may give a clue as to what is coming up will help reduce the number of unnecessary applications of the brakes and enable the speed to be maintained at a higher average. To achieve high road averages, it is essential first of all to concentrate on avoiding unnecessary braking and it certainly takes a lot of concentration before this becomes a natural habit. But while it saves time, it also helps to save tires, brakes and fuel. It can confidently be said that the merit of a driver is inversely proportional to the number of times he applies his brakes unnecessarily for a given mileage.

Passing on the Road

There are few occasions where foresight and good judgement can save as much time as when passing other cars on the road. Coming up behind a slower vehicle, where the road is not wide enough for three cars to be driven abreast safely, you first have to make the decision whether you can pass safely, or if oncoming traffic will force you to slow until the road is cleared. Once this important decision is taken, and if you have decided to stay behind, it is very important accurately to judge the speed of the other two vehicles and adjust the progress of your car in such a way that you come up behind the vehicle to be passed at the highest possible speed, just at the moment when the oncoming vehicle has cleared the road.

The earlier you slow down, the less your speed will have to be reduced and the quicker your former cruising speed can be regained. Having no control over the speed of the other two vehicles, the spot where they will pass each other is a predetermined point and the faster your speed when you pull out to pass, the better the run-in you get into the next stretch of road. If you do not reduce speed soon enough, you will have to brake down to a slower speed, maybe even down to the speed of the vehicle to be passed, and then pick up from that speed as the road is cleared. If, thanks to good judgement, your former cruising speed of 100 miles per hour is reduced only to 80 before you can pick up again, it will take a good sports car only about 5 to 7 seconds to regain its former cruising gait; if bad judgement compels you to slow down to 30 miles per hour before you can pick up again, it will take about three times the time to regain the original cruising speed. Such quite unnecessary losses of 10 to 20 seconds quickly add up to several minutes and may well spell the difference between keeping to a tight schedule or not.

Foresight may also help save the car and the suspension system from se-

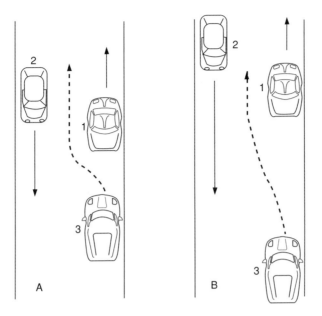

Fig. 70.   *Passing with oncoming traffic.*
              A Incorrect   *B correct*

vere road shocks such as may be caused by pot-holes, a gully running across
the road or a hump-back. Such hazards may be difficult to recognize sufficiently early to check the speed to a rate where the car will run over them
smoothly; or you may have to maintain too tight a schedule to permit slowing down as much as you would like. Nevertheless, you must remember that
braking increases the load on the front suspension, which must bear not
only an increased weight, but also the brake torque reaction. Braking also
creates a nose-dipping movement that reduces the upward travel of the
front suspension and its ability to absorb road shocks. The suspension
should therefore be relieved of all additional strain induced by the action of
the brakes, by releasing the brakes just before it is called upon to absorb a
severe shock. It is even possible to time the release of the brakes in such a
way that the rebound of the suspension resulting from it increases the upward range of travel of the wheels at the precise moment when it is most
wanted for the absorption of the impact. In this way a car can be made to

jump an obstacle to a certain extent.

Foresight and observation will also enable you to drive fast and safely on the open road where visibility is scanty. Where the road disappears beyond the crest of a hill or a major hump, trees or telegraph poles, or in some countries advertisement boardings, may give you a clue to the direction it takes where it cannot be seen and enable you to place the car correctly to negotiate the stretch fast and safely. Nearing the crest of a rise, you may come up behind another car which it does not seem safe to pass because the crest may be hiding a vehicle coming in the opposite direction. The answer may well be given by road users travelling in the same direction as yours. If, for example, some way beyond the crest the roof of a car preceding you can be seen, you may assume that if a vehicle were coming in the opposite direction you should also see its roof and that it is therefore safe for you to pass. Or if on the crest of a hill or leaving a blind corner, a driver in front pulls out to pass, you may assume that the road is free and do so yourself. Even if the other driver has acted wrongly, his car will serve you as a protecting screen against any oncoming traffic. And, of course, difficult roads winding up or down the side of a mountain can often be observed over quite long distances, so that the opportunity should never be lost to spot vehicles coming the other way and to be prepared to make room for them when the time comes.

Safety Belts

If safety belts have, in some cases, been found responsible for killing, there is no question that, statistically speaking, the chances for the occupants of a closed car of escaping injury or worse in a serious accident are very much reduced if they wear properly adjusted seat belts. Contrarily to general belief, wearing a belt is possibly more important in city traffic than on the highway. A 30 mph head-on collision can easily be fatal if no belt is worn but, at least in a modern car, is certainly not if a belt is properly worn. But the chances of survival in a head-on crash at even only 70 mph are virtually nil, whether a belt is worn or not.

For racing, a six-point harness is compulsory in most disciplines, tying the driver (and in rallies the co-driver) down in the seat, preventing him or her to move forward or to the side. In conjuction with a roll-over cage in a closed car, or roll-over bars in open cars, this ensures not only the maximum possible protection, but also the best possible comfort in fighting centrifugal and braking forces which, with the down force generated by the aerodynamic devices, can reach very high levels.

Chapter IX

How To Become a Racing Driver

A racing career can be started in many different ways and the stories of the rise to fame of the foremost racing drivers would no doubt make interesting and varied reading. Very few of them appeared right out of the blue; for the majority the road leading to the cockpit of a first-class racing car was a long and strenuous one.

Today, most of the top drivers started racing go-karts at an early age, long before they could acquire a driver's license. Karting is a perfect and not excessively dangerous way of learning to control a racing car (what a kart is, on a small scale), to get the "feel" for the lines to be taken and for the limits of adhesion, and to learn all the tricks which make racing what it is. From karts, the most current way of graduating is to go to one or the better known race driving schools, most of which are sponsored by oil companies. The cars on which the pupils are instructed are usually single seaters of a minor formula, providing the proper environment and, to round up the courses, a competition is usually organized between the pupils, in which the lesser gifted are eliminated until it comes to the final in which six candidates compete for the yearly title with which usually comes a racing car with enough money for a complete season's racing, while second prize in most cases also takes the form of a worthwhile sponsorship.

Of course, you can also go directly to the racing school, without going through karting, but in the school, those with previous karting experience have a considerable advantage, which may mean that, to have a chance to reach the final at the end of the stage, you must stay in the school for two successive years.

There are obviously other ways of getting into racing, one of them being one-make racing of which there are many variants, either for single seaters like Formula VW, Formula Ford or Formula Opel-Lotus, or for production based cars like the Renault 5 Cup, Peugeot 309 Cup and others. No particular qualification is required to apply for participation in those one-make races and the necessary competitions license is delivered by the national body governing motor sport following a medical examination. It should however be stressed that participation in races for closed body, production based cars is not recommended to those whose target is racing "open wheel" single seaters as

a) the environment is completely different;

b) pure racing cars are much more responsive than production based sedans;

c) most single make production derived cars have front wheel drive and consequently behave quite differently from pure racing cars.

Unless you have a rich friend prepared to sponsor your early efforts, it will cost you quite a lot of money and usually a lot of time before you find yourself sitting in a race car on the starting grid of a racing event. If you can't muster either the time or the money, you can surely get fun in taking part in club events or national hill climbs in which there are always classes for relatively inexpensive cars, from more or less pure production models to second or third hand small racing cars which are not competitive any more in international races, but which can still achieve results in lesser events.

Fig. 71. A hard fought Formula 1 race in hot weather is a very exhausting exercise, as reflected by Nigel Mansell's expression after the Spanish Grand Prix of 1990 in which he finished second to his Ferrari team mate Alain Prost.

Once you have made the grade, the best way to improve your ability is to race as much as possible. Not only is practice indispensable, but it provides an opportunity to observe other, more experienced drivers. But do not enter races in which you or your car would almost surely be hopelessly outclassed. This is asking for trouble and you would only make a nuisance of yourself. Even Formula 3 racing has now become too professional an affair for a beginner to enter, unless he has gained previous experience in other forms of competition or in a racing drivers' school.

Money spent on a race-driving course or school is never wasted. The least expensive of these organizations are those in which the pupil drives his own car, which should be a reasonably fast vehicle if the course if to be really worthwhile. These courses usually last for two or three days, which is not long enough for big improvements in one's ability to handle a car to be expected, but during this time much food for thought is given to the participants which they will assimilate over a longer period, when their driving will become progressively better.

This is the sort of school aimed essentially at the enthusiast anxious to improve his driving, but who has no aspiration to become a racing driver.

That the only really efficient way of learning how to handle a car under racing conditions is actually to race it is obvious, because nowhere other than on a track can the car be driven at its limit and along a line that will enable it to take full advantage of the available width of road. It is surprising how much the judgement of even the most gifted driver with no racing experience, and the accuracy with which he handles his car, will improve with racing practice. On the other hand, I do not agree with those who say that driving on ordinary roads is no help in keeping a driver in racing fettle. True, those highly professional drivers who spend three or four days of nearly every week in the cockpit of a racing car, either racing, practising for races or testing the cars, will benefit much more from some rest while they are away from the tracks than from covering huge mileages on the roads. But I believe that for a person who races less frequently, to use a fast car on long journeys on fast roads, far from the bulk of traffic and from insidious "radars," keeps him or her in the habit of travelling fast and helps retaining good judgement of braking distances and high cornering speeds as well as keeping reflexes sharp, even though braking and cornering performances of today's road cars are much inferior to those of racing cars.

It must however be stressed that there is a vast difference between fast driving on the road and dangerous driving, and though they usually average quite phenomenal speeds from point to point, racing drivers worthy of the

Fig. 72. Taking Arnage corner, the author demonstrates the driving position he advocates in his victorious drive of a Ferrari at Le Mans in 1960.

Fig. 73. Olivier Gendebien and Paul Frère being fêted after driving a factory-entered Ferrari Testa Rossa to victory in the 1960 Le Mans 24 Hours race.

name are very safe on the road, where they can call upon a judgement trained at much higher speeds and under more exacting conditions than those prevailing on ordinary roads. Their quest for speed, and their need to express their ability to its utmost, are satisfied by their racing activities, under fully controlled conditions and with a minimum of incidental risks. They can see no reason for taking chances—at crossroads, at blind corners, or in overtaking. After all, if you can hold your own among the pick of the world's racing drivers on the track, there is very little point in trying to match your skill against that of any unknown driver of a family sedan, or even sports car, that you may meet on the road.

Given but moderate ability, they can always leave you behind by taking the sort of chances that must sooner or later end in disaster.

Chapter X

DOs and DON'Ts

DOs:
Remember that no book can teach all aspects of driving and racing. There is no substitute for attending qualified driving schools and learning to drive and race under controlled, safe conditions.

Start racing at the lowest possible level so that you can assess your own ability compared with other people's and waste the minimum amount of money if there is little hope of getting anywhere.

If you don't prepare your car yourself, spend as much time as you can with the mechanics who prepare it for you, so as to get as much knowledge as possible of its anatomy. Every car has its weak points, and it is best to know what they are so that you may drive accordingly. It may also help you diagnose any possible abnormality in the car's noise or behavior during the race, and thus to decide whether to stop or to press on.

Keep an eye on what other people do before the race and an ear open for what they say, particularly if they are more experienced than you are, and look for interesting details of their cars. They may give you useful hints.

If you are your own manager, write down full details of the practice and race conditions: the lap times, fuel consumption, the state of tune of the car, the gear ratios, the tire pressures, the kind of fuel and oil used, the oil pressure and temperature, the water temperature during the practice runs and the race, and so on and so forth. These notes may be very useful at a later date, especially if you return to the same circuit with the same car or one which is basically similar.

Before you start practicing and before the start of the race, make quite sure that someone present in the pits knows your blood group and rhesus.

Wear light, narrow shoes. They will help you operate the pedals with precision.

Make sure you know where the knob operating the fire extinguisher is located in the cockpit.

Make sure that the driving position is exactly as you want it; especially if the race is a long one, nothing must be neglected to make yourself really comfortable. Use padding to prevent bruises whenever necessary.

Be sure to memorize where the ignition switch is, and which way it must be operated to stop the engine should the throttle fail to shut.

If it rains or is likely to rain, sew a small leather on the back of your gloves to easily wipe your visor.

If you realise that the engine has died or cannot be started in time for the start of the warm-up lap or the race, raise your arm so that officials and drivers behind you understand that your car cannot move and act accordingly.

If the engine is not equipped with a revolution limiter, it is very easy to over-rev in the first few hundred yards after the start, when you have to watch the other cars running in close attendance and you can hardly recognize the sound of your engine from theirs. Take great care that you don't, it could be expensive, besides costing you the race.

During the race, try to drive a little faster than is enjoyable; you cannot go really fast without frightening yourself occasionally.

Pay very careful attention to any oil that may have been left on the track by other cars.

If it starts to rain, slow down sufficiently not to take any risk, then increase speed progressively as you become familiar with the new state of the track.

Watch your rear-view mirrors as often as possible and occasionally have a quick glance behind at a hairpin, so as to judge the distance of your followers more accurately.

Be quite sure you know the meaning of the various flags, and watch for them during the race.

Be quite sure to remember that overtaking on the yellow flag is strictly forbidden and may lead to disqualification.

Be quite sure you know the regulations, especially those peculiar to the particular event. It is very important to know the exact starting procedure and the number of people who may work on the car during a pit stop.

Go early to bed the night before the race, and if you feel nervous, don't hesitate to take a sedative in order to get a good night's sleep.

Make an early start to the venue. Traffic conditions are likely to be difficult, and having to worry about getting to the start in time will strain your nerves even more than they already are before a race.

Make sure you have all the necessary passes to get to the paddock. The arguments that will otherwise ensue will also not improve the state of your nerves.

If you don't know the circuit, try to arrive in time to drive several times round it with a private car before the first practice session starts. This will enable you to take better advantage of the time provided for official practising and you will be less of a nuisance to others who already know their way around. Don't forget to look for possible escape roads during the reconnaissance.

From the length of the race and the average speed reached by the fastest cars during practice, calculate the approximate duration of the race. A glance at your watch will then give you a fairly accurate indication of how far the race has progressed. If you are not up amongst the fastest group of competitors, it may also be well worth while calculating how long it will be before the leaders are about to lap you, so that you can pay particular attention to keeping out of their way as they close up on you. It's a good way of getting popular with the top men.

DON'Ts:
Don't race or practice race driving anywhere except on a designated racetrack.

Don't drink any alcohol with, or after the meal preceding practice or the race, and avoid consumption of alcoholic drinks during the practice and race period.

Don't eat more than a light meal before the race.

Don't forget to carry your competitors' licence with you.

Always use a new or perfectly unscratched visor and leave a spare with a reliable person in the pits. If any rain is expected, don't forget to treat your visor with an anti-mist compound. Soap is as good as most of them.

Don't omit to keep an accurate check on fuel consumption and tire wear during practice.

Don't wait until the last moment to start the engine.

Don't wait for too long on the starting line with the clutch depressed.

Don't forget to properly adjust your driving mirrors before the start.

Don't forget to inform your team manager or a reliable person in the pit of your blood group and rhesus: this precaution may save your life in case of an accident.

Don't omit to read the race regulations and make sure you know any rule peculiar to the race concerned.

Don't wait until the last moment to wheel, or drive, your car to its proper starting position.

Don't pull your visor down too early when waiting for the start, it may mist up.

Don't forget to tell the people responsible for your signalling what sort of information you will be particularly interested in receiving.

Don't get in the way of faster competitors, but when they have overtaken you, try to keep up with them as long as you can and watch their methods closely: you can learn a lot this way.

Don't take anything a racing driver says for granted. Even the most reliable ones can only say what they think they do. If one tells you he takes a bend flat-out with a car similar to yours, and you do not, never try to do what he says without building up progressively to it. If he tells you he brakes at the 150 meter sign for a corner, try first at 250, then 200 and then reduce your distance progressively if you see it really can be done. Drivers usually consider they have reached a landmark when they see it at about 45 degrees to the car's centreline, not when they get level with it, which makes quite a difference. In addition, their instinct of preservation makes them apply the brakes a fraction of a second earlier than they actually think they do.

To do what a racing driver says he does without building up to it progressively, is the quickest way of getting killed.

If you decide to change your line through a fast bend, never do so without first trying the new line of a slightly reduced speed, to see if it is really better. It may be worse, in which case, you will be glad you reduced your speed. Only by sheer luck did I avoid a very nasty crash, at about 100 mph, by not observing this rule in one of my first big races.

Don't forget that, away from the normal line, the grip of a race track's tarmac is considerably reduced.

Don't change gear unnecessarily. Every gear shift costs nearly a car's length, so it may be better to stay in a higher gear than to change down to get momentarily better acceleration, and then change up again. In case of doubt, always stay in the higher gear, you will be faster and strain the car less.

Don't drive any faster than is necessary to achieve the best possible result you can hope for, while keeping a reasonable safety margin over the closest competitor. Of course, this can mean driving as fast as you possibly can all the way!

In a long-distance race, never eat anything heavy while waiting for your turn at the wheel, and get as much rest as possible. Before you resume driving, make quite sure of your car's position in the race, and how far in front or behind your most dangerous opponents are.

When handing over to your co-driver, don't forget to inform him of any abnormality in the car that has come to your notice, especially where the brakes are concerned, and also report them to the team or pit manager.

Never wear any item of nylon clothing or clothing of similar material that will melt in the case of a fire.

134

DON'Ts

The Effect of Banking Angle and Tire Load on Maximum Cornering Speed

L et us assume that, for a given radius of the curve, the centrifugal force F_c is equal to the weight W of the vehicle. In this case, if the lateral components created by these two forces are to cancel each other out, as happens if the car is driven along the correct line around the banked curve, the banking angle must be 45 degrees.

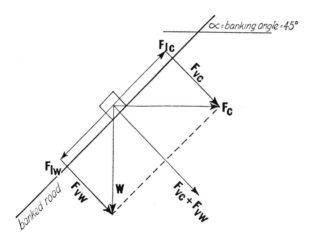

Fig. 74.

We have $F_c = \dfrac{mv^2}{r}$

v being the speed of the car in ft./sec, r being the radius of the curve. But we have assumed that $F_c=W$, and $W=mg$, m being the mass of the vehicle, and g being the acceleration of gravity.

For F_c to be equal to W, we must have

$$\frac{mv^2}{r} = mg, \text{ and } \frac{v^2}{r} = g.$$

Thus

$$v^2 = r\dot{g}.$$

Under these circumstances, the force with which the car bears upon the road surface is

$$F_{vc}+F_{vw}=F_c \sin \alpha + W \sin \alpha = \sin \alpha (F_c+W).$$

As in our case, $\alpha=45°$ and $F_c=W$, we have

$$F_{vc}+F_{vw}=0.71 \times 2W = 1.42W.$$

The total force with which the car bears upon the track is thus 1.42 times its own weight.

Let us now assume that the car's speed is increased to the extent that the centrifugal force F_c becomes twice the car's weight: $F_c=2W$, and let us calculate what the banking angle will have to be for F_{lw} and F_{lc} to be equal.

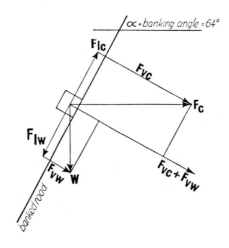

Fig. 75.

We have

$$\cos \alpha = \frac{F_{lc}}{F_c},$$

$$\sin \alpha = \frac{F_{lw}}{W}.$$

As $F_c = 2W$ and $F_{lw} = F_{lc}$, we have

$$\cos \alpha = \frac{F_{lw}}{2W}, \text{ and } \sin \alpha = 2 \cos \alpha.$$

It follows that

$$\sin^2 \alpha = 4 \cos^2 \alpha. \qquad (1)$$

By definition,

$$\sin^2 \alpha = 1 - \cos^2 \alpha. \qquad (2)$$

Subtracting (2) from (1), we have

$$4\cos^2 \alpha - 1 + \cos^2 \alpha = 0, \text{ or } 5\cos^2 \alpha = 1.$$

Thus

$$\cos^2 \alpha = \frac{1}{5} = 0 \cdot 20,$$

$$\cos \alpha = \sqrt{0 \cdot 2} \cong 0 \cdot 45$$

and $\alpha = 64$ degrees.

Thus, for the sideway forces acting upon the vehicle to cancel each other out, when the centrifugal force F_c is twice the car's weight, the banking must be inclined at 64 degrees to the horizontal.

As $F_c = 2W = 2mg$,

$$\frac{v^2}{2r} = g \text{ and } v^2 = 2rg.$$

and as $g = 32.18$ ft./sec.^{2}

$$v^2 = 64.36r, \text{ and } v = \sqrt{64.36r} \text{ ft./sec.}$$

137

Appendix I

$$v^2 = 19 \cdot 6r, \text{ and } v = \sqrt{19 \cdot 6r}.$$

At this speed, and at the correct banking angle of $\alpha=64$ degrees, the component of the centrifugal force acting perpendicularly to the road surface is

$$F_{vw} = F_c \sin \alpha = 2W \sin \alpha \cong 1.8W;$$

and the component of the weight acting perpendicularly to the road surface is

$$F_{vw} = W \cos \alpha \cong 0.45W.$$

The total force with which the car bears upon the road is thus

$$F_{vc} + F_{vw} = W \ (2 \sin \alpha + \cos \alpha) = 2.25W$$

or 2.25 times its own weight, in the circumstances described. This condition is reached at a speed of approximately 230 ft./sec. = 157 mph.

138

Appendix I

Appendix II

The Effect of Down Force on Maximum Cornering Speed

Neglecting aerodynamic factors, the speed at which, in theory, any vehicle can negotiate any given bend depends on only two parameters: the radius of the bend and the coefficient of adhesion of its tires on the road surface. The highest possible cornering speed is reached when the centrifugal force acting upon the vehicle equals the grip, resulting from the multiplication of the total vehicle weight by the coefficient of adhesion μ. The limit is independent of the vehicle's weight as both the centrifugal force and the grip are directly proportional to the weight.

If r is the radius of the curve in meters, v the vehicle's speed in meters/second (m/s), w the vehicle's weight in kg and m the vehicle's mass (m=weight/g with g=the acceleration of gravity = 9.81 m/s per second), the centrifugal force is:

$$F_c = \frac{m \cdot v^2}{r} = \frac{w \cdot v^2}{g \cdot r} \ (kg) \tag{1}$$

and hence:

$$v = \sqrt{\frac{r \cdot F_c}{m}} \ (m/s) \tag{2}$$

The limit of adhesion being reached when the centrifugal force $F_c = \mu \cdot W$, the highest possible cornering speed is given by the very simple equation

$$v_{lim} = \sqrt{r \cdot g \cdot \mu} \ (m/s) \tag{3}$$

This is valid as long as the grip remains constant irrespective of the vehicle's speed, which is seldom the case, due not only to the possible variations of the road surface (which, in this case, we shall neglect, assuming the surface to be near perfect and of constant grip characteristics) but also to aerodynamic lift.

Due to these aerodynamic forces as well as to other factors not taken into account by the formulae (such as tire construction, suspension characteristics, location of the center of gravity etc.), the actual possible cornering speeds can to some extent depart from the theoretical figures, but assuming a coefficient of adhesion $\mu = 0.85$ to 0.9 for good modern tires running on good asphalt, most modern cars can produce a centripetal acceleration (lateral g in motoring jargon) of anything between 0.8 and 0.9 g.

With Down Force Into Another World

Up to the late 'sixties, the cornering speeds of racing cars were only slightly higher than those of the best road going sports cars. The improvement resulted from a lower center of gravity, more handling oriented suspensions and the higher grip of racing tires which were not required to last as long as road tires. But it is doubtful whether Formula One cars and sports prototypes of the pre-1967–68 years were able to corner at anything superior to 1.1 g. The radical change came when racing cars first grew spoilers and airfoils and, in 1977, when Colin Chapman came up with the Lotus 78, the first "wing car" in which the ground effect was exploited to create enormous down force at a comparatively small expense of drag.

FISA tried to minimize the benefits of the down force producing devices in order to stop the vertiginous rise of cornering speeds, by limiting the size of the airfoils, banning skirts and imposing a "flat bottom" between the front and rear wheels. But the fact remains that far from being subject to lift, as is the case of most road cars, modern racing cars are literally squeezed onto the road by an invisible aerodynamic down force which, at speeds around 300 km/h (186 mph) can exceed twice their own weight.

Racing tires have also made enormous progress: structures are better, rubber is much softer and the much increased sizes provide a larger "gearing" area with the road surface. Today $\mu = 1.7$ is a conservative figure for the coefficient of adhesion.

In order to illustrate the effect of modern tires and the huge down force produced by the combination of ground effect and airfoils, notwithstanding the limitations imposed by FISA, we shall take the case of a modern Formula One car in which the down force amounts to 1300 kg at 300 km/h (186 mph). This is a fairly conservative figure resulting from information gathered from a number of manufacturers. We shall also assume that the coefficient of adhesion of tire to road surface is a conservative $\mu = 1.7$. The minimum weight of a Formula One car, less fuel but otherwise in racing trim being 500 kg, we shall accept that the car with half-full tanks and the driver on board weighs 700 kg.

In this case, the weight is important as, while the centrifugal force remains a direct function of the car's weight, *the grip is proportional to the TOTAL force acting upon the ground*, i.e. *car weight PLUS down force*, the latter increasing as *the square* of the vehicle's speed.

Knowing that the limit of adhesion is reached when the centrifugal force equals the grip, the highest possible cornering speed in a curve of given radius is obtained by replacing F_c by $W+F_d$ in our formula (2) above, which gives:

$$v_{limit} = \sqrt{\frac{r\,(W + F_d)\cdot\mu}{m}} \qquad (4)$$

Assuming the down force to be 1300 kg (2866 lb) at a speed of 300 km/h (83.33 m/s or 180.4 mph) and knowing that all aerodynamic forces vary as the square of the relative air speed, we get:

Down force at 300 km/h (83.33 m/s or 186.4 mph): 1300 kg
Down force at 250 km/h (69.44 m/s or 155.3 mph): 903 kg
Down force at 200 km/h (55.55 m/s or 124.3 mph): 578 kg
Down force at 150 km/h (41.67 m/s or 92.2 mph): 325 kg
Down force at 100 km/h (27.78 m/s or 62.1 mph): 144 kg

For $\mu=1.7$, the maximum cornering speeds on a perfectly level road can be deducted from formula (4):

Curve of 50 m radius: v=32.5 m/s = 117 km/h (72.7 mph)
    Corresponding lateral acceleration: 2.15 g.
Curve of 100 m radius: v=54.8 m/s = 197 km/h (122.4 mph)
    Corresponding lateral acceleration: 3.07 g.
Curve of 150 m radius: v=86.4 m/s = 311 km/h (193.2 mph)
    Corresponding lateral acceleration: 5.04 g.

The figures only indicate what can be expected for a given airfoil settings, but these can be modified to suit different circuits. On slow courses, the airfoil incidence would be increased to produce even more down force at any given speed, while on very fast circuits it would be reduced to avoid excessively penalizing the maximum speed and high-speed acceleration. It must also be remembered that when the car is driven through a turn, the air stream is no longer fully parallel with the car's longitudinal axis, which slightly reduces the efficiency of the devices generating down force.

The enormous grip provided by the down force also helps braking performance. In a road car, the best retardation that can be expected lies around

1 g resulting from actual braking plus air drag. The latter obviously increases at high speeds, but the advantage obtained from increased drag at high speeds is usually compensated for by reduced grip resulting from higher lift forces. In racing cars both the drag and the down force increase as the square of speed and, provided the brakes themselves are powerful enough, they combine to increase the retardation at an even quicker rate than the cornering force as speed increases: at speeds around 280 km/h (approx. 175 mph), retardation can be as much as four times higher than for a road car.

In the light of such performances, the cornering speeds of even the best road going sports cars look fairly pathetic, as the following table shows. In this, we have assumed that the road going car has zero lift (which is rather exceptional) and that it rolls on modern high performance tires of which μ on dry asphalt is of the order of 0.9.

Radius of curve	Racing Car	Road Car
r = 50 m	73 mph	47 mph
r = 100 m	122 mph	66.5 mph
r = 150 m	193 mph	81.4 mph

Appendix III

The Effect of All-wheel Drive on Handling

T o analyze the handling characteristics of a 4-wheel driven car, we shall exclude all the factors influencing the handling, except the 4-wheel drive. Consequently, we shall assume that with no drive transmitted, the car has a completely neutral cornering behavior. Consequently the front and rear slip angles are equal and we assume the car's mass to be equally distributed between the front and rear axles.

When a wheel rolls freely (without transmitting a driving force), its adhesion to the road surface is equal to its load multiplied by the coefficient of friction μ.

$$F_{ad} = \mu \times Load$$

It is also known that a force applied at right angle to the plane of a rolling wheel induces lateral slip and that the slip angle increases as the lateral force increases. *The larger the slip angle, the smaller the margin of adhesion left before the slip turns into slide.* It follows that the slip angle is a measure of the margin of the remaining grip available to resist lateral forces.

The slip angle (and consequently the grip margin) depends on both the lateral force acting at a right angle to the wheel and on the driving force transmitted by the wheels of the axle concerned.

Lateral force and driving force are linked by the formula:

$$\text{Available grip} = \sqrt{\mu P^2_{axle} - F^2_d}$$

with P_{axle}=weight born by the axle and F_d=driving force.
It follows that the margin of grip or adhesion can be influenced by the two factors:
1. The driving force.
2. In the case of the front wheels of a rear wheel driven car, by the component of the driving force always directed along the longitudinal axis of the car, acting perpendicularly to the plane of the front wheels which, in a turn, forms an angle with the car's longitudinal axis.

In the case of rear- and four-wheel driven cars, the handling characteristics are influenced by both these factors. In front-wheel driven cars, only the first factor intervenes.

The curves of available grip have been calculated for a car having the basic characteristics of the original Audi Quattro for average front wheel locks of 7 and 24 degrees and grip coefficients $\mu=0.83$ and $\mu=0.3$.

It can be seen from the curves on the following pages that for a given driving force a 4-wheel driven car has a larger front wheel grip margin than a front-driven car in all situations likely to be experienced. This means that it understeers less.

Because of the weight transfer under acceleration, a rear-wheel driven car also tends to understeer if the front wheel lock is large and the driving force moderate. A high driving force reduces the understeering tendency and eventually produces "power oversteer." The shorter the wheelbase and the higher the center of gravity, the more the car tends to understeer and the more power is necessary to create oversteer.

Most cars with permanent 4-wheel drive are fitted with some device that automatically and rigidly links the front and rear pairs of wheels in case wheel spin sets in. On low-μ surfaces, such as snow, ice or earth, this makes it possible for the driver to power the car through the turn in a controlled drift. The four wheels follow the direction of the resultant of the two components: lateral force and driving force. This explains why, even in a 4-wheel drift, the front wheels remain turned in the direction of the curve, unless the driver must unwind the steering because he has made a mistake.

For readers interested in the calculations:

1. Lateral grip margin $\Delta F_L = \sqrt{\mu F_L^2 - F_d^2}$

2. ΔF_L in rear-driven cars:

Front axle: $\Delta F_{Lf} = \mu P_f - \dfrac{F_d \times h}{W} - F_d \sin \alpha$

Rear axle: $\Delta F_{Lr} = \sqrt{\left(\mu P_r + \dfrac{F_d \times h}{W}\right)^2 - F_d^2}$

144

Appendix III

3. ΔF_L in front-driven cars:

Front axle: $\Delta F_{Lf} = \sqrt{\left(\mu P_f - \dfrac{F_d \times h}{W}\right)^2 - F_d^2}$

Rear axle: $\Delta F_{Lh} = \mu P_r + \dfrac{F_d \times h}{W}$

4. ΔF_L in 4-wheel drive cars:

Front axle: $\Delta F_{Lf} = \sqrt{\left(\mu P_f - \dfrac{F_d \times h}{W}\right)^2 - \dfrac{F_d^2}{4}} - \dfrac{F_d}{2}\sin\alpha$

Rear axle: $\Delta F_{Lr} = \sqrt{\left(\mu P_f + \dfrac{F_d \times h}{W}\right)^2 - \dfrac{F_d^2}{4}}$

Difference: $\Delta F_{Lf} - \Delta F_{Lr}$ $-=$ Understeer
$+=$ Oversteer.

Symbols: P_f = Weight on front axle; P_r = Weight on rear axle.
F_d = Driving force; F_L = lateral force.
h = Height of center of gravity
W = Wheelbase
μ = Coefficient of adhesion
α = Average lock angle of front wheels

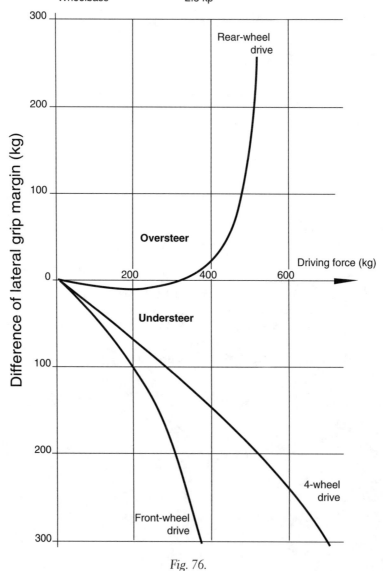

Fig. 76.

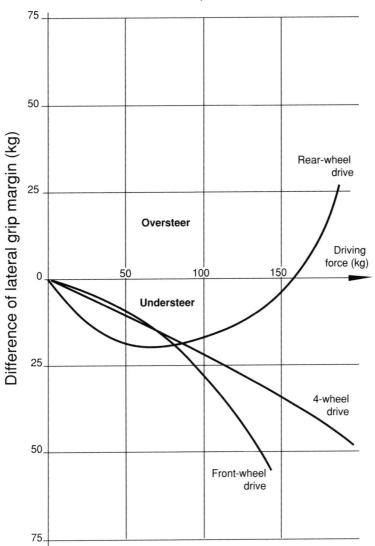

Steer angle (average α = 24°, μ = 0,3)
(Snow, dirt)

Total vehicle weight	1200 kp
Weight on front axle	600 kp
Weight on rear axle	600 kp
Height of center of gravity	0.4 kp
Wheelbase	2.5 kp

Fig. 77.

Appendix III

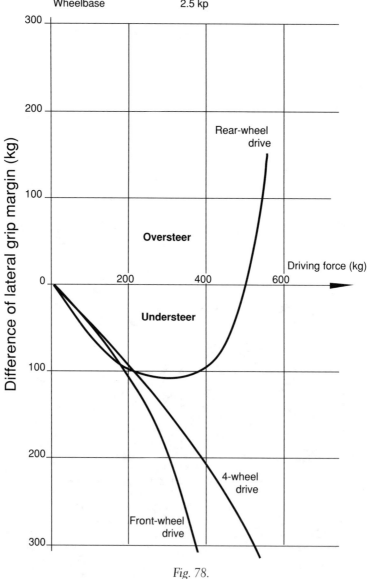

Steer angle (average α = 24°, µ = 0,8) (Asphalt)

Total vehicle weight	1200 kp
Weight on front axle	600 kp
Weight on rear axle	600 kp
Height of center of gravity	0.4 kp
Wheelbase	2.5 kp

Fig. 78.

Index

Note: numbers in bold type indicate
  Figure numbers
Acceleration, Maximum 19, 26, 84
Accelerator 18, 33: **13**
Accidents 111 ff: **65**
Adhesion, Front-wheel drive 67
Adhesion, Tire 35, 36, 44, 53, 65: **33,**
  53
Aerodynamic aids 70 ff: **45**
  airfoils 77, 80: **45**
Aerodynamic tuning 80, 81
Alcohol 132
Angle, Drift- 61 ff: 41, **43**
  Yaw- 64, 65, 68: **38, 40, 41**
Anticipation 112
Anti-glare mirror 121
Anti-mist compound 89
Anti-roll bar 74, 79
Ascari, Alberto 112
Aston Martin DB3S **64**
Austin-Healey **18**
Automatic transmissions 22

Banked bends 45 ff., 83: **32, 30**
Banked tracks 48 ff: **30**
  dangers of racing unsuitable cars on
  50
Banking 45
  angle and tire load 135 ff: **74, 75**
Baulking 107, 108
Belgian Grand Prix 121: **15**
Bend, Drifting a car through a 62 ff:
  39-43
Bend, Banked 45: **28, 30**
Bend, Correctly engineered 47: **28**
Bends, Succession of 45 ff: **26**

Bianchi, Luciano **34**
Blood-group 130, 132
Bonetto, F. 121
Brabham, Jack **50, 51**
Brake-fade 24
Brake fluid 24
Brakes
  Disc- 24
  Anti-lock 26
  linings 25
  pedal 12, 26
Braking 24 ff., 67, 123
  and speed 121, 122
Braking distance 25
  on wet circuit 116
B.R.M. car **16**

Camber 46: **27, 28**
  Adverse 47
Camber, Road, taking advantage of
  46 ff: **29**
Camber, Wheel 53, 74
  effects of negative 74: **63**
Caster adjustment 76
Centrifugal Force 35, 36, 42, 47, 145:
  22, 23, 30
Chart keeping 93: **58**
Circuit, Learning the 82, 132
Circuit racing 31, 33, 34, 84
  practicing 82 ff.
Claes, Johnny 121
Clark, Jim **16**
Clothing, Racing 88, 89, 134: **52, 54**
Club racing 126
Clutch pedal 18, 103, 104, 132
Co-driver, Handing over to 134

Collins, Peter **64**
Collisions 112 ff., 124
   Multiple 113, 114
Communication
   and time keeping 91 ff.
   Radio- 99 ff: **58, 59**
Competition Licence 125, 132
Cooper-Climax **10, 50, 51, 61**
Corner, Driving into and out of a 41 ff.
Cornering 35 ff., 82 ff: **10, 14-21, 24-26, 29-30, 42, 50, 51**
Cornering speeds
   in rain 115
   of racing cars 145 ff.
Curve
   of constant radius 36 ff: **17, 20, 21**
   decreasing radius **47**
   increasing radius **48**
   irregular radius **49**
   S-bend 45: **26**
   variable radius 38: **19-21**

Dallara **66**
Deduction 113
Double de-clutch 18, 26
Down force 72, 78, 146: **45**
Drift angle 61 ff: **39-43**
Drift, Four-wheel 32, 33: **41, 51**
Drifting a car through a bend 62 ff: **37, 40, 50, 51**
Driving in rain 115ff., 131: **70**
Driving position 14 ff., 133
   correct **2, 3, 6, 7**
   incorrect **4, 5, 8**
   with safety harness **9**
Duez, Mark **71**

Emergency line 114 ff: **67**
Engine, Minimum wear-and-tear on 20
Escape area 82

Fangio, Juan Manuel 101, 112, 121
Farina, Dr. G. 112
Ferrari
   1955 Grand Prix **15**
   1958 Le Mans **11**
   1960 Le Mans **64, 72**

Fire extinguisher 130
Fireproofed clothing 88, **52**
Flags 108 ff., 131
   black 110
   blue 108, 109
   chequered 110
   green 109
   red 110
   red and yellow striped 110
   white 110
   yellow caution 111, 131
Flag marshals 108 ff.
Flockhart, Ron **61**
Food before a race 132, 134
Foresight, Value of 122
Formula I racing 101: **71**
   III racing 127
   Ford 125
   Opel-Lotus 125
   VW 125
Four-wheel drive car
   and four-wheel drift 33: **43**
   winter driving 119
French Grand Prix 50
Frère, Paul
   driving "Indy" March-Porsche on Nürburgring Grand Prix course (1989) **57**
   driving Porsche turbo **38**
   in Cooper-Climax **10**
   in Jaguar D-type at Le Mans (1957) **1**
   in Ferrari (1955) **15**
   in Ferrari at Le Mans (1960) **64, 72**
   instructing Porsche driver at driving course **29**
   Le Mans in poor weather conditions **44**
   testing Mazda 787 at Paul Ricard Circuit **46**
Front lights 121
Front-wheel drive
   Cornering with 67
   and four-wheel drift 33
   Disadvantages of 67
Front-wheel slide 42: **23**
Fuel 93
   consumption 19, 87, 93, 102, 130, 132

Gear-boxes 18, 85
Gear, changing 18 ff., 133
Gear-ratios 84, 85, 130
Gearing 84 ff.
Gendebien, Olivier
    driving position of **11**
    on banking at Montlhéry **30**
Ginther, Richie **16**
Gloves 88
Go-karts 125
Goggles 120
Gonzales, J. F. 121
Grand Prix Racing Start 103

Handling characteristics **16**
    of 4-wheel driven car 139 ff.
Hawthorn, Mike 114
Headlights 121
"Heel-and-toeing" 26 ff: **12, 13**
Helmets **54, 58**
Hill, Graham **16**
Hill, Phil **50, 63**

Ice, Driving on 119
Ignition switch 131
Inertia forces 41
Instruments 120: **59**
Italian Grand Prix (1953) 114

Jaguar D-type **1**

Landmarks 83, 124
Lap chart 93
    times 93, 94, 130: **56**
Lauda, Nicki 100
Le Mans Circuit 27, 108, 112: **11**
    Start **62**
    Twenty-Four Hours Race **65**
Lewis, Jack **61**
Line, The 35 ff, 82 ff
    emergency 114 ff: **67**
    transitory 44: **25**
Lotus car **16**

Mairesse, Willy **34**
Mansell, Nigel **71**
Marshals, Flag 108 ff.
Maserati 112, 121

Maximum acceleration 19, 26
    economy 20
    performance 19
    torque 20
May, Michael 70
Mazda 787 **46**
Mille Miglia 30
Minimum wear-and-tear 20
Mirrors
    Driving 107, 131, 132
    Anti-glare 121
Monte Carlo Grand Prix 112: **14**
Monte Carlo Rally 68
Montlhéry Circuit 48
    Gendebien's Ferrari on the banking
        at **30**
Monza Circuit 112
"Moss Line, The" **16**
Moss, Stirling 112
    in Lotus during 1961 Monte Carlo
        Grand Prix **14**

Negative wheel camber, effect of 74
Night, Racing at 98, 120, 121
Nose dipping 123
Nürburgring 82
    Thousand Kilometer Race 70
Nylon clothing, Dangers of 134

Oil pressure
    gauge 120, 130
    thermometer 120
Outbraking 104
Overalls 88: **52**
Over-revving 131
Oversteer 55 ff., 74, 79, 80, 140: **35-37,
    40, 42**
Oxygen **54**

Passing, 104 ff., 122ff: **70**
Peugeot 309 Cup 125
Pit organization 93
    signals 93 ff.
    stops 93: **64, 65**
Polar inertia 42, 43
Porsche racing car **29**
"Power oversteer" 60, 61, 142: **38**
Practice times 101

Practice 82 ff.
　Pre-race 30, 132
Prost, Alain **39**

Qualifying 87 ff.

Race, The 88 ff., 103 ff.
　calculate length of 132
　nervousness 88, 131
Race-driving schools 125 ff.
Racing
　clothing 88, 89: **52**
　Club- 126
　DOs and DONTs 130 ff.
　driver, Becoming a 125 ff.
　Road- 30
　tactics 100 ff.
　time sheet **56**
Radio communication 99 ff: **57, 58**
Rain, Racing in 115 ff., 131: **68**
Rain tires 91
Rally driving 30, 112 ff.
　in winter 119
Rear-wheel driven car
　and four-wheel drift 33
　cornering **42**
Rear-wheel slide 44
Re-fueling stops 87, 93
Regulations 131, 132
Renault 5 Cup 125
Revolution limiter 104, 131
Rev counter 120
Rheims Circuit
　French Grand Prix **50**
Rhesus factor 130, 132
Road book 30
Road camber, Taking advantage of 46 ff
Röhrl, Walter 33
Roll stiffness 73, 74

Safety 111 ff., 128, 133: **66**
Safety harness **9, 66**
Seat belts 124
Seat, Driving 12
　Height of 18
Senna, Ayrton **25, 55**
Shock absorbers 74

Shoes 130
Signalling 93 ff., 133
　panel, illuminated 98
Skid, correcting 54
Slide, Front-wheel 42: **23**
　Rear-wheel 42
Sliding 53
Slip-angle 52, 137: **32**
Slipping 51 ff: **31, 32**
Slipstream, Taking advantage of 87, 101, 107
Snow, Driving in 119
Spa Circuit 101
Speed and safety 111 ff: **66**
Speedometer 120
Start, The 103 ff: **60-62**
　Grand Prix 103
　Le Mans-type **62**
　rolling 104
Starting position 132
Steering 55 ff.
　wheel 12, 13, 17, 44, 70, 71: **2-6**
　　grip on 13: **7, 8**
Stewart, Jackie 100
Studs, Tire 77
Suspension 73, 75, 77 ff.
　braking and 123
　springing and damping 77 ff.

Tactics, Racing 101, 102
Taylor, Trevor **62**
Team managers 130
　signals 95, 98
Theory and practice 73 ff.
Thermometers 120
Time keeping 91 ff.
Time sheet **56**
Tire adhesion 35, 36, 42, 53, 65: **33, 53**
　load, Banking angle and 135 ff.
　pressures 52, 90, 130
　qualifying 87
　Rain- 91
　sizes, effect of different 76, 77, 87
　slip-angle of 52
　snow- 91
　temperature 90
　wear 25, 90, 132: **53**
Tires, choice of 90 ff.

Toe-in and toe-out (wheel) 74, 75
Torque 20 ff., 44
Tour of Corsica 32
Transitory turn 44 ff: **24, 25**
Transmission, Automatic 22
Trips, Wolfgang von **50**

Understeer 55 ff., 65, 66, 74, 79, 80,
140: **35-37, 50, 69**
  turning into oversteer 59 ff: **40**

Visibility, Fast driving with restricted
118, 120: **68**
  Importance of perfect **57**
Visor 89, 118, 131, 132, 133

Water thermometer 120
Weight distribution 76
Wheel
  camber 53, 74
    effects of negative 74
  lock 25, 26
  sizes 76, 77
  spin 25
  toe-in and toe-out of 74, 75
Winter driving 119

Yaw angle 64, 65, 68: **38, 40, 41**

153

Index

Photo Credits

Courtesy of Aston Martin Lagonda Ltd.
Fig. 59

Courtesy of Phillipe de Barsy
Figs. 9, 25–26, 39, 45–46, 52–55, 66, 71

Courtesy of Geoffrey Goddard
Fig. 63

Courtesy of Louis Klemantaski
Fig. 14

Courtesy of John Lamm
Fig. 38

Courtesy of Max Pichler
Fig. 29

Courtesy of Porsche
Figs. 42, 57–58

Courtesy of Jean-Louis Taillade
Fig, 68

Courtesy of Toyota
Fig. 69

Courtesy of Andre Van Bever
Figs. 1, 10–11, 15–16, 18, 30, 34, 44, 50–51, 60–62, 64–65, 72–73

The photographs listed on this page are copyrighted by the providers and are used by permission.

The remainder of the illustrations were prepared by P. Weller.

About the Author

Paul Frère was born in 1917 and educated in Brussels as a commercial engineer. He began his racing career in 1946 on motorcycles, but soon moved into automobiles and first drove in competition in the 1948 Spa 24 Hours Race, in a prewar PB-type MG, finishing 4th in class and 15th overall. Over his distinguished career Frère has had 11 first-place finishes in Spa production car races alone, in such diverse automobiles as Panhard, Oldsmobile, Chrysler, Alfa-Romeo, Jaguar, Aston Martin and Porsche.

In the 1953 Mille Miglia, driving a Chrysler, Frère was 1st in the over-2-liter Touring Car class. Also in 1953 at Le Mans he was 1st in the 1500cc class and 15th overall. In 1955 at Le Mans he was 2nd overall and first in class driving an Aston Martin. In the same year he was 4th in the Belgian G.P. in a Formula 1 Ferrari and was named Champion of Belgium for the year. In 1956 Frère was 7th in the Drivers World Championship.

Frère seemed to have a special affinity for Le Mans, driving to 4th overall in 1957 (Jaguar), 1st in class and 4th overall in 1958 (Porsche 1500), and 2nd overall (Aston Martin) in 1959. He crowned his driving career in 1960 with 1st at Le Mans in a Ferrari, driving with Olivier Gendebien, 1st in the South African G.P. (Cooper) and 1st in the Spa Sports Car Race (Porsche).

Frère has been writing as a journalist as long as he has been racing, since 1946, using his unique viewpoint as both championship driver and engineer to produce articles about automotive and technical subjects. He still pursues his love of driving and writing today, as European Editor for *Road&Track* Magazine.